How to Mess Up Your Child's Life

PROVEN STRATEGIES
& PRACTICAL TIPS

Olivia and Kurt Bruner

NEW YORK   BOSTON   NASHVILLE

Unless otherwise noted, Scripture is taken from the HOLY BIBLE, NEW INTERNATIONAL VERSION®. Copyright © 1973, 1978, 1984 International Bible Society. Used by permission of Zondervan. All rights reserved.

The "NIV" and "New International Version" trademarks are registered in the United States Patent and Trademark Office by International Bible Society. Use of either trademark requires the permission of International Bible Society.

Scriptures noted KJV are taken from the King James Version of the Bible.

Scriptures noted ESV are taken from The Holy Bible, English Standard Version, copyright © 2001 by Crossway Bibles, a division of Good News Publishers. Used by permission. All rights reserved.

FaithWords
Hachette Book Group
237 Park Avenue
New York, NY 10017

Visit our Web site at www.faithwords.com.

Printed in the United States of America

First Edition: March 2009
10 9 8 7 6 5 4 3 2 1

FaithWords is a division of Hachette Book Group, Inc.
The FaithWords name and logo are trademarks of Hachette Book Group, Inc.

Library of Congress Cataloging-in-Publication Data
Bruner, Olivia.
    How to mess up your child's life: proven strategies & practical tips / Olivia and Kurt Bruner.—1st ed.
        p. cm.
ISBN: 978-1-931722-77-3
    1. Child rearing—Religious aspects—Christianity.   2. Parenting—Religious aspects—Christianity.   I. Bruner, Kurt D.   II. Title.
    BV4529.B795 2009
    248.8'45—dc22   2008038112

TO OTIS AND GAIL LEDBETTER

Your example and coaching kept us out of many a mess!

Contents

※

Introduction

It's All Downhill

Few careers must be less satisfying than selling exercise equipment. Oh, sure, you might rake in big bucks during the first ten days of January when most of the population makes its annual "get fit" resolution. Selling Bowflex and ThighMasters to a pudgy population can be great if you believe the gear will actually get used. But it can't be rewarding earning commissions February through December on products gathering dust in the corners of garages—taking up space rather than sculpting shapes, creating guilt-induced shame instead of muscle-bound frames.

Sadly, we can relate to the feeling because the same thing happens to those of us who write parenting books. Inspired in a fleeting moment of good intentions, many parents buy our advice. But we fear very few put it into practice.

So, tired of watching our advice gather dust, we decided to tackle the issue from a slightly different angle. We dared to ask the obvious question: *why does so much great parenting advice go unheeded?* The answer, it turned out, brought us back to lessons learned way back in the earliest days of Sunday school. Those lessons now form the basis of what we call our "theology of kids."

You see, the Christian faith tells us we are made in the image of God with tremendous capacity for goodness, joy, success, and healthy living. Imagine our original ancestors standing atop an unbiased "scale of freedom" with their Creator pointing them toward a potentially wonderful existence and away from the problems that come with rejecting the good for which He made us.

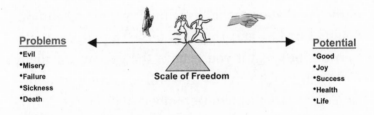

Problems
•Evil
•Misery
•Failure
•Sickness
•Death

Scale of Freedom

Potential
•Good
•Joy
•Success
•Health
•Life

Being made in the image of God means every one of us has the potential to become a saint. That's the good news.

But there is also some bad news. Grandpa Adam and Grandma Eve made a choice that infected the human bloodline with a disease called *sin*. They turned their backs on their potential and predisposed all of us to vices like rebellion and laziness.

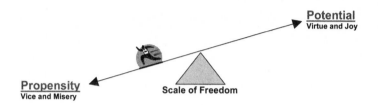

That's why doing what's right is so much harder than doing what's wrong. Reaching our potential for virtue and joy is like turning around and climbing a very steep hill. (In fact, the word *repent* means to turn around and go the other way.) With no effort at all, however, we can speed toward vice and misery.

In this context, we realized that the problem with most parenting books is their tendency to point up a steep hill and shout "Climb!" to those who want to do a good job with their kids. Rearing successful children requires much more grit and determination than many of us feel we can muster. And so, unheeded parenting advice sits on millions of bookshelves right next to millions of unused aerobic videos.

That is why we've decided to break away from the pack of parenting experts, daring to defy conventional wisdom. Rather than try to motivate moms and dads to climb a steep incline of parenting methods that might produce successful and happy children, we thought it high time someone offered an alternative voice.

So, you hold in your hands the first-ever guide to messing up a child's life, offering timeless wisdom and proven strategies for parents who want to go with the flow rather than resist the current, and who prefer a leisurely walk to an exhausting climb. In other words, the kind of advice that's easy to implement because it aligns with our natural bent.

Assumptions

Let's begin with a summary of some basic assumptions behind "mess-up" parenting:

ASSUMPTION #1: EVERY CHILD IS AT RISK OF BECOMING SUCCESSFUL AND HAPPY

Ask ten people their definition of success and you might get ten different answers. Some will describe a career or financial goal, others will talk about the importance of family relationships, while still others might point to great athletic accomplishment.

Funny, we don't seem to have the same problem when we make the question more specific. Asking ten people to define success for a hammer, for example, will likely trigger some variation of the same response. "Driving nails into wood." We immediately recognize success for a hammer as fulfilling the purpose for which it was made. Name any object, and you will see the same pattern:

- What is success for a television remote control? Changing the channel.

- Success for a blender? Blending.

- Success for an aspirin? Easing pain.

You get the idea. In every other context, we define success in terms of purpose. Good parents do the same for their children: give them a framework for life such as this one from the book of Ecclesiastes: "Fear God and keep his commandments, for this is the whole duty of man" (12:13). Or the words of Jesus, who said, "Love the Lord your God with all your heart and with all your soul and with all your mind. This is the first and greatest commandment" (Matt. 22:37–38).

Believers throughout history have used creeds and confessions to give their children a sense of purpose, such as this from the Westminster Confession of Faith: "Man's chief end is to glorify God, and to enjoy him for ever."

A child is dramatically more likely to achieve success when parents explain the purpose for which he or she was made. Mess-up parents, by contrast, let their kids grope for some sense of purpose on their own. That's why so many former children come to the end of life and discover that they have been leaning their "success ladder" against the wrong wall.

Yes, every child is at risk of achieving the purpose for which he or she was made and discovering the happiness that comes with success. But mess-up parents can mitigate this risk by keeping their children occupied with more trivial concerns.

ASSUMPTION #2: EVERY CHILD IS BORN WITH TREMENDOUS CAPACITY FOR MESSING UP

When our oldest son, Kyle, hit age two, he fell in love with a little book called *All Mine, Bunny*. Each night for several months Kyle toddled over to one of our laps with *All Mine, Bunny* in hand and implored us to once again read "dis one" before tucking him into bed. Children love repetition, even if parents prefer a bit of variety in their reading selections. But we didn't mind. After all, *All Mine, Bunny* dealt with why we should share—a very important subject for any toddler.

After several months of following that bedtime pattern, we invited another couple who were parents of a toddler to our home for dinner. As the four adults enjoyed dinner in the dining room, the kids played in the next room. Much to our delight, we overheard Kyle say the word "share." A few minutes later, we heard him say it again—prompting us to smile and wink at each other, knowing our reading ritual was paying dividends in the life of our firstborn.

The third time, we could no longer contain our pride. "Excuse us," we said, "but we need to take a look at what's happening in the next room."

Just in the nick of time, Kurt peered around the corner to observe Kyle shouting the word "Share!" in a very demanding tone as he forced a toy out of the other toddler's hands.

We are like balls living on a slant. The pull of our nature rolls down to selfishness and self-destruction. That's why trying to move children uphill toward their potential success and happiness requires intense effort. Mess-up parenting, on the other hand, is a simple matter of letting them roll.

ASSUMPTION #3: EVERY PARENT HAS THE SKILLS NECESSARY TO MESS UP A CHILD'S LIFE

Each and every parent walking the planet started life as a child. And every child, as we've already discovered, has the capacity for messing up. So, even if your own parents helped prevent your ball from rolling very far downhill, you still have what it takes.

The key, of course, is reaching deep for what psychologists call "the inner child"—that part of you that never really grew up. You see, each time we suppress a selfish impulse or sacrifice our own desires for a child's well-being, we inadvertently turn the trajectory of parenting uphill rather than downhill. As creatures of habit, we can quickly develop patterns that become difficult to break:

- A father getting out of his La-Z-Boy chair to play catch with his son.

- A mother reading bedtime stories to her small children rather than relaxing in a bubble bath.

- Parents who drive their kids to church on Sunday morning instead of driving themselves to the country club for a game of tennis.

- Driving a used car so you can afford to pay for your kid's braces.

- Biting your tongue at dinner table spills instead of biting your child's head off.

- Caressing a child's forehead while he or she leans over the toilet bowl at midnight.

Such patterns, left unchecked, make it far more difficult to mess up a child's life. But deep down, we all have a selfish, lazy nature eager to impact the next generation!

ASSUMPTION #4: CONVENTIONAL WISDOM POINTS UPHILL

Virtually anywhere you go for parenting advice, from a family sermon at church to a Dr. Phil special on television, you will hear the same basic mantra. In fact, you probably recognize many of the following phrases:

- Be sure to balance love and discipline.

- Establish and communicate clear rules and boundaries.

- One of you needs to be the parent in the relationship.

- Good parenting takes a lot of hard work.

Read the Bible and you will discover similarly intimidating admonitions:

- Train a child in the way he should go. (Proverbs 22:6)

- Discipline your son, and he will give you peace; he will bring delight to your soul. (Proverbs 29:17)

- Do not exasperate your children; instead, bring them up in the training and instruction of the Lord. (Ephesians 6:4)

Do you notice the common thread? That's right. The Scriptures and conventional wisdom point only uphill. Both make the major assumption that we parents are willing to place the best interests of our children first. They expect us to do what's hard instead of easy, to go against our natural tendencies and to choose the noble path. Making matters worse, the Bible seems to expect the same of our children:

- Children, . . . honor your father and mother— which is the first commandment with a promise— that it may go well with you. (Ephesians 6:1–3)

- Children, obey your parents in everything, for this pleases the Lord. (Colossians 3:20)

Few kids come out of the womb eager to honor or obey. Ours came out looking for a fight.

Since both parents and children dislike forcing themselves uphill against their natural bent, we seek to offer much-needed inspiration. Adopt Bobby McFerrin's motto—"Don't worry. Be happy!" After all, it takes far less effort to roll than to climb.

ASSUMPTION #5: SOME CHOICES CAN UNDERMINE RAISING A TRULY MESSED-UP CHILD

Remember, because every child is made in God's image, he or she is at risk of becoming successful and happy. We must be on guard against the kind of parental choices and patterns that can seriously hamper the effort to raise a messed-up child. If we don't resist the urge to do the right thing, we can throw a wrench in the entire plan. That is why we've included a section in each chapter called "Taking Precautions," which highlights examples from those who have messed up the "mess-up" process. Pay special attention to these segments in order to avoid repeating the same mistakes.

Seven Habits of Highly Defective People

Each chapter of this book draws upon a long tradition of biblical understanding about the choices and patterns that accelerate a child's downhill momentum. We've chosen the seven "habits" that dramatically increase the odds our kids will mature into highly defective people. Tradition calls them *the seven deadly sins.* *Deadly*—not like dropping dead upon first offense, but like a terminal illness that gradually kills our capacity for real life. You could also call them *vices* or *character flaws.* No matter what label you put on them, however, the basic list has remained pretty consistent for hundreds of generations. Orthodox Christianity defines them this way:

1. *Pride*—The lack of humility befitting a creature of God

2. *Envy*—Jealousy of some other person's happiness

3. *Anger*—Unworthy irritation and lack of self-control

4. *Gluttony*—The habit of eating or drinking too much

5. *Greed*—Too great a desire for money or worldly goods

6. *Sloth*—Laziness that keeps us from doing our duty to God and humanity

7. *Lust*—Impure and unworthy desire for something evil

Each of these vices has an opposite virtue freeing us from its bondage. Pride, for example, is overcome through humility. Greed is defeated by generosity, lust by chastity. You get the idea. These seven could be seen as the collective gravitational pull that keeps humanity rolling downhill, the root causes behind a wide range of related sins too numerous for a single list.

Why these seven and not others? Because Christian history views most other sins as the sprouting branches of these seven. As British author Henry Fairlie explains in his book *The Seven Deadly Sins Today*:

> The deadly sins are all leashed together, and
> it is this that is emphasized in the traditional

classification. There are not simply all the individual sins we can count, of which we are guilty in one degree or another, there are these seven capital sins that lie deeply rooted in our natures. Faced by the description of them, we know that we elude none.[1]

For generations the "deadly sins" have created the context within which all human beings, including your children, will make choices that move them toward success or failure. In short, we either climb up or mess up.

Benefits

We recognize that some moms and dads might not be sure they want messed-up children, especially when tempted by books with more inspiring titles like *Ten Steps to Raising Successful Offspring* or *Helping Your Kids Reach Their Potential*. So we thought it might be a good idea to mention a few of the many benefits associated with choosing this approach to parenting.

BENEFIT #1: AVOIDING DISAPPOINTMENT

Let's face it, you won't find a more common source of disappointment in people than unmet expectations. We all have children who, despite our best efforts to instill character and common sense, will make their own choices. And some of the choices they make can break a parent's heart. Why set yourself up for such a letdown? Messed-up parenting fully expects children to roll downhill. It even encourages the process. So if they hit bottom—no surprise!

BENEFIT #2: ESCAPING THE COMPARISON TRAP

If you've ever attended an elementary school awards ceremony, brought your son to a Little League team tryout, or participated in a church-sponsored Bible memory contest, you know how humiliating it can be when a neighbor's kid outperforms your own. And then there are those times your child throws a temper tantrum in the middle of the grocery checkout aisle, prompting every other parent in your zip code to stare that unspoken condemnation of your inferior parenting skills. Mess-up parents refuse to play that game, removing themselves entirely from the comparison trap. One can be made to feel like a failure only if he or she cares to succeed. Don't.

BENEFIT #3: BE LIKED RATHER THAN RESPECTED

Every parent wants to be a friend to his or her children. But conventional wisdom places a high priority on parents' commanding respect and maintaining a position of authority in the relationship. Rather than live with the tension, however, mess-up parents simply abandon the role of authoritarian. Just like that,

Mom and Dad can begin focusing 100 percent of their energy on keeping the peace. All the stress and strain associated with expecting and maintaining respect dissipates as the "let's be pals" priority prevails in each and every situation.

BENEFIT #4: NO "HIGH HORSE"

Few things are more obnoxious than people who give parenting advice even when they have not been asked. Nobody likes listening to a dad describing his own perfect kids or a mom pointing out mistakes we've made with ours. Thankfully, mess-up parenting keeps you off such a high horse because you aren't likely to recommend your own approach to others, nor is anyone likely to seek your advice.

BENEFIT #5: A VAST POOL OF EXPERTS

Mess-up parents can be found everywhere you look. Literally billions of moms and dads have trailed a path before us. Together we will learn from that vast pool of "experts" who have chosen the road most traveled— the wide path instead of the narrow gate.

In the book of Proverbs, Solomon describes the heart of a child as something "bound up" with folly. He goes on to say that "discipline will drive it far from him"

(22:15). In other words, he or she has the potential to outgrow foolishness if well trained. That, in a nutshell, summarizes the uphill and downhill realities of parenthood.

For mess-up parents, this means the less effort put forth, the better. The momentum of folly can quickly overtake every area of a child's life if we simply get out of the way and let it happen—an approach to parenting we further explore in the following chapters.

For those not quite sure they want a messed-up child, we ask that you maintain an open mind. Why not invest a few hours ignoring the promise of successful, happy children in order to discover the possibilities of a parenting approach that demands little of you and less of your kids? Join a growing network of moms and dads who have discovered the freedom and child-rearing results available only to those not really trying.

How to Mess Up
Your Child's Life

CHAPTER ONE

Nurturing an Enormous Ego

(Deadly Sin: Pride)

Not one more step!" ordered the little boy's mother.

Halted in his tracks, the preschool lad peered back over his shoulder from the front porch steps. He had intended to make an escape and explore the wide, wonderful world of Louisville, Kentucky, their hometown. Sure, dangers abound. Of course, young children are supposed to remain in the protective care of a house under the watchful eye of a mom and a dad. But such rules apply to ordinary kids—not kids destined for greatness.

His gauntlet thrown down, their eyes met. Yet another clash of wills was under way, and neither side intended to lose.

"You heard me," insisted the mom. "Don't you dare take another step!"

And without saying a word, young Cassius glanced back and forth between the next step and his mother's threatening glare. A decision had to be made. Back off, or accept the challenge?

"Cassius!" The stern tone suggested she was in no mood for mischief. If he just turned his little bottom around and walked back into the house, he could avoid a whole heap of trouble. But that would mean losing a battle . . . or what's worse, swallowing his pride.

So he took a single step. Just one. That's all that was needed to make it clear that he, not she, was in control. Cassius had a reputation to establish, the promised spanking and early bedtime a small price to pay.

In March 1963, the face of that same little boy was plastered on the cover of *Time* magazine. A mere twenty-one years old, Cassius Marcellus Clay had been calling himself "the greatest" for years. People who knew him thought he talked too much. Some called him the "little smart aleck" with a ton of potential. He threw his first punch as a small child, knocking out his own mother's tooth.[1] Years later, his punch won him an Olympic gold medal and the world heavyweight championship.

Of course, he made many calculated choices along the way similar to the one made on that Louisville front porch. Every challenger had to lose, any obstacle overcome. Even if doing so meant hurting others. After all, greatness requires sacrifice.

He quickly sacrificed respect for others, taunting his challengers with derogatory names like "that big ugly bear." He also gave up the trainer who helped him achieve Olympic greatness, trading up to one he considered "top-notch."[2]

Cassius Clay eventually even gave up his name, adopting the more commonly recognized label Muhammad Ali. *Cassius Clay* connected him to his father and race. He and his dad had been named after the famous nineteenth-century abolitionist,[3] rooting his identity in the struggle for freedom among former slaves, something he abandoned in favor of a new religious identity called the Nation of Islam led by his spiritual mentor, Malcolm X. Cassius's new first name, Muhammad, meant "one worthy of praise."[4]

What kind of "praise" did such sacrifices solicit? Well, according to *Time*, sportswriters coined names for him like "the Louisville Lip," "Mighty Mouth," and "Cassius the Brashest." And half of those who purchased tickets to his fights hoped to see "the loudmouth get his comeuppance." Others practically considered it a moral obligation to root against Clay because nobody likes a loudmouth and they figured "Prideful Cassius was due for his fall."[5]

Such reactions are to be expected from those who fail to understand true greatness. And they rolled off of the champ's back like water off a duck.

"I'm beee-ootiful," he confidently shouted over such criticism. "I'm the greatest. I'm the double greatest."[6]

And to think he got that way one step at a time.

A Universe of One

While few parents want their children to ignore common courtesy or abandon their families and religious identities, all of us want them to become champs at some life pursuit. But we must face facts. Not many of us have kids with the talent or work ethic to win the heavyweight boxing title or any other world title for that matter. Nevertheless, we can still help them become the greatest in the universe. How? By doing what it takes to nurture an enormous ego.

You see, pride—when grown out of proportion—equips a child to become the center of his or her own universe. And in a universe of one, any child can be the greatest!

Richard Dawkins has emerged in recent years as one of the world's most famous atheists. He has written books with such provocative titles as *The God Delusion* and *The Blind Watchmaker* as he champions the notion of a world without any Supreme Being who makes demands upon our individual autonomy. In fact, one of his earlier books, titled *The Selfish Gene*, offers an indirect compliment to our selfish inclination. You see, the survival of the fittest, the theory that undergirds

Dawkins's worldview, depends upon each living organism "looking out for number one" and our genes existing for the sole purpose of benefiting themselves.[7] In other words, even our genes drive us to become gods of our own little domains.

Dawkins and a chorus of others who reject the idea of a personal God have helped lay an entirely new foundation for rearing the next generation. Old-school parenting took its cues from religion, seeing a single universe with one, all-powerful Lord over all. Christians believe that God even described Himself as "meek and lowly in heart" and went so far as to humble himself "by becoming obedient to the point of death, even death on a cross" (Matt. 11:29 KJV; Phil. 2:8 ESV). (No wonder conventional wisdom tells us to discourage pride and encourage humility.)

How liberating for parents and children alike to discover that being selfish should be seen as a gene-influenced virtue rather than a sin-infected vice.

Conventional Wisdom

Before diving into mess-up parenting strategies for nurturing an enormous ego, we need to spend some time trying to understand what conventional wisdom tells us about pride, which is commonly described as the first of seven deadly sins. The Scriptures certainly take a dim view:

- When pride comes, then comes disgrace, but with humility comes wisdom. (Proverbs 11:2)

- Pride goes before destruction, a haughty spirit before a fall. (Proverbs 16:18)

- A man's pride brings him low, but a man of lowly spirit gains honor. (Proverbs 29:23)

- For everyone who exalts himself will be humbled, and he who humbles himself will be exalted. (Luke 18:14)

- God opposes the proud but gives grace to the humble. (James 4:6)

Even the dictionary defines *pride* in mostly negative terms, including "an overhigh opinion of oneself" and "haughtiness" followed by "arrogance."[8] Hardly attractive associations.

Not surprisingly, then, conventional parenting advice encourages us to nurture virtues that fall on the opposite end of the continuum from selfishness and arrogance. Dr. James Dobson, for example, wrote *the* book for parents of self-centered children titled *The Strong-Willed Child*. In his updated version, *The New Strong-Willed Child*, he encourages moms and dads to "shape the child's will" without breaking his or her spirit. How? By disciplining childhood defiance while rewarding respectful attitudes and selfless behaviors[9]—in other words, by moving children away from the "vice" of pride.

To be honest, many of us struggle with the idea of calling pride a *vice* at all. Aren't we supposed to help children feel good about themselves, take pride in a job well done, pull themselves up by their own bootstraps, and overcome every limitation? Sure, some manifestations of pride can seem ugly. Yes, self-centered arrogance can hurt others. But we are, after all, only human. Right?

Only Human

Who decided to label pride a *sin* anyway? Don't all human beings, including our untainted children, have this "selfish gene" built into their DNA? Isn't this genetic disposition something natural to be nourished rather than something wicked to be curbed?

Those who advocate conventional wisdom respond with an unequivocal *No!* To justify their perspective they point to something Christian theology calls "original sin."

You see, selfishness and arrogance are indeed part of human nature. But just because something is natural does not mean it is necessarily good. Tornadoes are a natural phenomenon. That doesn't mean we celebrate when one strikes our home. Tooth decay is natural. But we still brush our teeth to prevent cavities and the eventual (dare we say *natural*?) toothache.

Remember what God told our first parents in the Garden of Eden: "You are free to eat from any tree in the garden; but you must not eat from the tree of the knowledge of good and evil, for when you eat of it you will surely die" (Gen. 2:16–17).

Offering a dissenting opinion, Lucifer tempted Adam and Eve by suggesting, "You will not surely die." Then, like a lawyer speaking legal jargon rather than everyday English, he gave a more technical interpretation: "For God knows that when you eat of it your eyes will be opened, and you will be like God, knowing good and evil" (Gen. 3:4–5).

Of course, the devil did not mean "know" as in hearing about it on the radio. He meant "know" as in intimate, personal, experiential knowledge. We can gain textbook knowledge about the law of gravity from a book. But we really *know* gravity when we experience a broken leg after falling from a tree.

The Fall, which occurred after picking fruit from a tree, caused our first parents, and the rest of us who inherited their genetic code, to break a leg. We didn't want anyone else, not even God, telling us to be careful—placing limits on our lives. So we walk with a limp. And a big part of that limp is our tendency toward pride and its unattractive children: arrogance, vanity, conceit, egotism, boastfulness, and selfishness.

So, says conventional wisdom, the deadly sin of pride became part of human nature. Natural? Yes. Good? Not so much.

Why Deadly?

What is so "deadly" about pride anyway? To answer that question, we revisit assumptions one and two.

"Every child is at risk of becoming successful and happy." Remember, hammers are made for nailing. Children, and the adults they eventually become, are made for God. The connotations of the word *death* include separating ourselves from our intended purposes. Instead of useful tools in the hand of a creative genius, we lock ourselves away in solitary isolation and begin to rust.

"Every child is born with tremendous capacity for messing up." The sin of pride is at the root of rebellion. In fact, the fall of humanity in Eden was simply a matter of our deciding to join Lucifer in his effort to throw off God's authority. Like a branch cutting itself off from its life-sustaining roots, we triggered a gradual process of deterioration that makes us less than fully human.

Do you remember Gollum from J. R. R. Tolkien's The Lord of the Rings trilogy? Perhaps the most pitiable character in all of literature, Gollum slunk his way through a self-consumed, self-destructive life, creeping through the dark shadows of a world of lost potential. You see, the pathetic, lizardlike creature once shared the same nature and potential as his hobbit companions Frodo and Sam. Smeagol, his original name, could have become heroic, like Frodo Baggins. He had the capacity to become loyal and selfless, like

Sam Gamgee. Instead of the god of his own smelly universe, Gollum could have been a humble, noble being. But his clutching after the power and control afforded by a magic ring turned him away from potential to the downward slope of evil. And as a result, he became less—much less—than he was made to be.

Sin can be described as anything we do that mars, mauls, inflates, depresses, distorts, or abandons our humanity.[10] And nothing better undermines achieving what we were made for than denying our Maker by making ourselves god.

"I will make myself like the Most High!" proclaimed the original Gollum (Isa. 14:14). "You will be like God, knowing good and evil," he said when tempting us to join his downward march.

Death is the opposite of life. It's not the end of existence but the beginning of something far worse: an eternity of madness and decay, separated from the Source of sanity and health.

A Lesson from Socrates

Conventional wisdom on this topic finds an ally in the ancient father of philosophy himself, Socrates. As described in Plato's *Apology*, Socrates spent much of his life asking questions of those around him who were considered wise. He approached powerful politicians, wealthy businessmen, great writers, and spiritual leaders, hoping to discover someone who could answer life's most basic questions. When none of them demonstrated the wisdom they claimed to possess, they became upset with Socrates. They accused him of being a know-it-all and wanted him punished for a trumped-up charge. But Socrates did not claim to possess the answers to the questions posed. He did not pretend to be wise. In his words, "I was conscious that I knew nothing at all . . . they certainly were wiser than I was."[11]

Recognizing his own ignorance, Socrates sought to learn from "the wise" by asking them questions. Doing so, however, revealed their ignorance, which in turn made them angry. "This inquisition has led to my having many enemies of the worst and most dangerous kind," explained Socrates while on trial for his life. "And I am called wise, for my hearers always imagine that I myself possess the wisdom which I find wanting in others: but the truth is, O men of Athens, that God only is wise; and by his answer he intends to show that the wisdom of men is worth little or nothing."[12]

Socrates captured the core of conventional wisdom in dealing with human arrogance and pride. God alone is wise, and only those humble enough to seek and acknowledge His superiority find answers to life's most important questions. Those who see themselves as the source of great brilliance are, in short, rather foolish.

So, where did such thinking get Socrates? Shortly after this wonderful speech the Athenian council sentenced him to death as "an evildoer," labeling him "a curious person who searches into things under the earth and in heaven."[13]

Mess-Up Strategies

Conventional wisdom points to the wisdom of Socrates, while the Bible quotes both Solomon and Jesus to discourage us from feeding a child's ego. But are these really the examples we want to uphold for our children? After all, Solomon wrote what must be the most depressing book ever penned, which begins "Vanity of vanities; all is vanity," and points out the emptiness of a life defined by stuff, pleasure, and power—the very things most of us chase (Eccl. 1:2 KJV).

Socrates ended up being condemned to death because people disliked the "better than thou" superiority a humble, teachable spirit can project. The fact is, most people consider themselves pretty doggone brilliant. They have no interest in some "evildoer" pointing out the folly of that opinion.

Jesus called His followers to "take up a cross" by dying to self (see Matt. 16:24). That could mean going to a foreign mission field or working in a soup kitchen rather than a law firm. He even called the poor in spirit "blessed" (Matt. 5:3). He is hardly a model of the kind of aspirations or ambition most parents want to instill in their children.

Who will offer alternative advice to those who want

to nurture an enormous ego in little Johnny or little Susie? We suggest three strategies.

MESS-UP STRATEGY #1: INDULGE SELFISH IMPULSES

From his or her earliest days, your child will show signs of being self-centered and demanding. Doing what comes naturally, children throw temper tantrums, hit one another, hit Mommy or Daddy, throw toys, throw food, take what they want when they want it, and scream in agony any time they hear the word *no*.

As they get older, kids move beyond childish demands to far more serious selfishness. They begin to resent any limitations, even those established for their own well-being. They will want you to butt out of their business, stay out of their way, give in to their demands, and pay for their desires. You might even hear them singing the words to Billy Joel's classic hit song "My Life": "Go ahead with your own life, leave me alone!"

Mess-up parents don't become uptight over such tendencies. In fact, they indulge them. When little Johnny slaps Mommy across the face or when Susie Preteen screams, "I hate you!" when told she can't have her own cell phone, conventional wisdom tells parents to discipline the wrong behavior. But mess-up parents know better, realizing it is much easier to give in. Discouraging a child's selfishness requires far more work for the parent than the child. To do that we must clearly define limits on their attitudes and behavior, followed by consistent enforcement of those limits year after year after exhausting year.

We get tired just thinking about all that effort. So seriously consider this innovative new motto: "Just Say Yes!"

MESS-UP STRATEGY #2: ENCOURAGE SELF-ADORATION

Successful parents tend to shower their children with praise. That's because conventional wisdom encourages us to give our kids a healthy sense of self-worth, reminding them of their value as people made in the image of the Creator. Conventional wisdom says to remind children of their tremendous capacity for good and to express admiration whenever your children work hard to put their God-given talents to use. Mess-up parents take this idea much further, encouraging children to admire themselves regardless of how bad they may have been or how little they may have accomplished. After all, if praise from Mom and Dad is good, admiring oneself must be even better.

Ancient mythology offers a wonderful example of this principle in the handsome Greek youth named Narcissus. Spurning the love of a goddess, Narcissus fell madly in love with his own reflection in a pool of water—eventually achieving immortality as his name became a term commonly used to describe vanity, egotism, conceit, selfishness, and snobbery.

Old-school parents tried to avoid narcissism and instill character in their children by attaching words of affirmation to proper behavior, hard work, or good attitudes. Mess-up parents, on the other hand, reinforce their children's narcissism by sending a different message.

- You are so good-looking!

- Yes, sweetie, you are the smartest kid in your class.

- You can skip practice, son. That will give the rest of your team a chance to catch up to your superior skills.

When we focus on praising children's effort and character, we point them toward success. By encouraging them to look in the mirror and take credit for what God gave them—such as their looks, intelligence, or talent—we give them a permanent gift. We help them remain infatuated with themselves regardless of how lazy or wicked they may become.

MESS-UP STRATEGY #3: ADAPT TO THE CHILD'S REALITY

Remember, you can guarantee that your child will become "the greatest" only if he or she inhabits a universe of one. This means you must adapt yourself to the child rather than expecting the child to adapt to you. It also means expecting others to adjust to the child's desires and demands rather than asking the child to respect someone else's schedule, needs, or expectations.

In the film *The Departed*, the voice of Jack Nicholson opens the story with a line that captures the true spirit of pride that his character, Frank Costello, embodies: "I don't want to be a product of my environment. I want my environment to be a product of me."

How do we foster such an attitude in our kids? Perhaps a few practical examples will help spark your thinking:

Give your children a free ride at home. They should not be expected to chip in by doing chores, helping with the dishes, or keeping their bedrooms clean. You do it for them to keep them from feeling responsible for their wider community.

Rescue your children from failure. If your daughter receives a bad grade after failing to study for a test at school, blame the teacher for being biased against her. If your son gets pulled from the starting lineup because he missed a few practices, protect his fragile ego by pulling him off the team to protest the "injustice."

Let them win the battles. When the inevitable conflict arises between what you need the child to do and what the child wants to do, back down. Let her finish the movie she started watching at nine o'clock even if her bedtime should be nine thirty. Allow him to keep playing his video game through dinner. He can always eat a snack later. Each battle won reminds your children that they are entitled to life on their own terms.

We should note that this strategy works easiest when you have an only child in the home. Adapting everything to your child's reality becomes far more challenging as you add additional children to the family. You can't necessarily prevent them from bumping into one another's expectations, and you want to give each an equal opportunity to rule his or her own universe. That's why larger mess-up families tend to follow this simple rule of thumb: the older the child, the less adapting to others. After all, rank should come with privilege. Especially in a universe of one.

Taking Precautions

In addition to implementing the recommended strategies, parents who want to mess up a child's life should try to avoid the mistakes of those who tend to nurture successful, happy children. Keep in mind, every vice that can be encouraged has an opposing virtue that might be nurtured. For those determined to mess up their children's lives by fostering the deadly sin of pride, increase your odds by ignoring the following ideas designed to instill the opposing virtue of humility.

> ### *WARNING:*
> *The following ideas could be hazardous to*
> *the process of messing up your child's life.*
> *Read at your own risk!*

WHY OBEY?

Part of overcoming self-centered pride is learning to submit to authority. We must choose to submit or suffer the consequences for failing to do so. In order to reinforce the protective nature of obedience, try these activities:

1. Have the kids draw a picture of people under an umbrella. Write the word *obey* on the umbrella to represent obeying authority, including parents, God, and others. Draw strong rain coming down around the umbrella, representing the hard knocks of life we experience when we take ourselves out from under God's protective instructions.

2. Pull out a real umbrella and have the kids get under it with Mom while Dad stands above them on a ladder or chair. Have several soft objects (rolled-up socks, Nerf balls, etc.) to drop on anyone who steps out from under the um-

brella. (If you conduct this activity outside, you may want to use a water gun!)

3. Use a stick or a string to create a line on the floor. Place a bowl of goodies several large steps beyond the line. Tell the kids they will be fine as long as they do not cross that line. When they do, nail them with the soft objects!

Once you've had some fun, read 1 Samuel 15:23; Exodus 20:12; and John 14:15 together and discuss the ways our lives are better when we learn to be obedient to the authority God places over us.

FOLLOWING DIRECTIONS

Tell your kids that you have planned an exciting outing to someplace special. You may or may not choose to reveal the destination, but make it a place you know they enjoy such as a favorite restaurant, ice-cream shop, mini-golf center, a bowling alley, or a movie theater. Create a special map that has step-by-step directions to the location. Assign a child to help you navigate. (If your child can't read, let him or her simply point which way to go after the instruction has been read.)

As the child tells you which direction to turn, stubbornly ignore his or her instructions. Arrogantly proclaim that you know what you are doing and you don't need to heed the map. Your child will likely become very frustrated with you, insisting that you follow the directions so that you don't get lost. After several turns, stop the car and admit that you are lost. Give the kids a chance to scold you for failing to follow the map.

Ask the kids what you should do next. They will say go back to the start and follow the directions. This time, do as they say. Upon arriving at the special location, read 2 Timothy 3:16–17 and/or Psalm 119:105 and share that God gave us the Bible as a life map, and that those who are wise obey its directions—but the proud refuse to submit to God's loving guidance.

TURN AROUND

Part of accepting responsibility for and overcoming our prideful attitudes and actions is humbling ourselves through repentance. Here are some simple ways to help your children grasp the idea:

- In order to understand what it means to *repent*, kids must first understand what *sin* is. Set up several "hit the mark" activities, such as shots at a toy basketball hoop, hitting Dad with paper wads, a plastic bowling set, Nerf baseball, and so forth. One at a time, let the kids attempt to score as many points as possible. Each time they miss, however, yell the word *sin* without explaining why. After several such outbursts, they will likely ask you to explain why you are yelling *sin* each time they miss. Answer by reading Romans 3:23 and 6:23 and explaining that sin is "missing the mark."

- In order to explain the word *repent*, blindfold the children one at a time and tell them to walk in a straight line until they hear you yell *repent!* When they hear you yell *repent* they need to immediately turn around and start walking in the other direction to avoid running into the wall or something else. (For added fun, when Dad takes his turn he can ignore the shouts and run into the wall, demonstrating the consequences of refusing to repent.) Read Mark 1:4, 15 and explain that repenting is turning away from sin and going the other way.

In summary, when we do something wrong (miss the mark), we need to repent (turn around and go the other way).

GIVING RESPECT

Make a hard-and-fast rule in your home: *There is never an excuse for treating others with disrespect!* Demand that everyone in the family (including Mom and Dad) treat others with respect. No demeaning others, ignoring others, or making others feel unimportant. When

Mom or Dad asks that something be done, the kids are to respond in a respectful manner. When a sibling is sharing about his or her day, others are to listen with sincere interest. It is in these and other small matters in everyday life that we affirm the personal worth of each individual in the family and model how to treat others in the larger human family.

LOW-SCORE BOWLING NIGHT

Jesus taught His disciples to counter their tendency toward "looking out for number one" by becoming a servant. "If anyone wants to be first," He said, "he must be the very last, and the servant of all" (Mark 9:35). Because we are so competitive and want to push ourselves to the top, take the kids bowling and tell them the winner will be the person who gets the *lowest* score. (Note: The rule is that a gutter ball gives you ten points, so you can't simply throw ten gutters. It is best to use bumpers if available to prevent gutter balls.) After having fun trying to hit the *fewest* possible pins, discuss how much harder it is to strive to be last than it is to try to be first! This is much like human pride. We tend to want to be served rather than serve others.

THE VOYAGE OF THE DAWN TREADER

Read this wonderful adventure from The Chronicles of Narnia by C. S. Lewis, which highlights the problem of a self-centered attitude and the beauty of humility. In the story, Eustace's selfishness gets him turned into a monstrous dragon. His only escape is to endure the painful redemption of humility. (Note: A wonderful version of this story is available from *Focus on the Family Radio Theatre* for the entire family to enjoy listening to together. Visit www.radiotheatre.org.)

MOVIE NIGHT: *A RIVER RUNS THROUGH IT*

For older teens, this story by Norman Maclean puts a fresh spin on the old tale of two brothers, one generally compliant, the other a strong-willed prodigal. Though reared by the same loving mother and father, who is both a Presbyterian minister and a fly-fishing fanatic, the boys make very different choices for their lives—and experience very different outcomes. Touching and tragic, this film paints a clear picture of how choices bring consequences—good and bad. Here are a few questions to draw out the key lessons of this film:

> *Question:* Why did the younger brother (Paul) have a harder life than the older brother (Norman)?
> *Answer:* Because he made many foolish choices.

> *Question:* Given the choice between doing what is responsible or right and doing what is frivolous or wrong, which would Paul choose?
> *Answer:* Frivolous or wrong.

Question: Did these choices hurt anyone?
Answer: Yes, they hurt him and his entire family.

Question: What Bible verses does this story illustrate?
Answer: Galatians 6:7–8.

CHAPTER TWO

Inspiring Lasting Discontent

(Deadly Sin: Envy)

A half-crazed reclusive old man repeatedly screams his victim's name, pleading pardon for his murderous deed. Attendants rush to the room where a once-renowned but now long-forgotten musician sits in a pool of his own blood. Adding a botched suicide to his list of failures, the injured man is rushed to the local insane asylum for care and incarceration. A young priest slips in beside the recuperating inmate to hear his confession and offer absolution.

So begins the film adaptation of Peter Shaffer's brilliantly crafted play *Amadeus*. Set in eighteenth-century Austria, the story is built around the supposed friendship and rivalry between Wolfgang Amadeus Mozart and his contemporary Antonio Salieri.

In the play, Salieri is an average talent exalted to the honored position of court composer. His one desire in life is to achieve fame by creating beautiful music. And things go quite well, for a while. The king favors Salieri and his mediocre compositions, making him the most successful musician in the city of musicians. But then one day, Mozart comes to Vienna—and changes everything.

Title and status become hollow to Salieri because he knows himself vastly inferior to the younger composer. Salieri simply can't create the kind of heaven-inspired music that flows effortlessly from the heart and hand of Mozart. Angry at the God he considers unjust and cruel for giving him the ability to recognize but not create great music, Salieri points his finger at God and challenges Him to a duel. "So be it!" he prays. "From this time we are enemies, You and I!"[1]

Fueled by the desire to block God's voice, Salieri determines to destroy Mozart by burying his music and, if necessary, his corpse. "God needed Mozart to let Himself into the world. And Mozart needed me to get him worldly advancement. So it would be a battle to the end—and Mozart was the battleground."[2]

But Mozart dies before Salieri can implement his full strategy. God, it seems, has the victory. Over the ensuing years, the poison of bitterness consumes the inferior composer's mind, driving him to concoct one last stanza in order to pry a few scraps of lasting recognition from his divine enemy's clenched fist: "I cannot accept this. I did not live on earth to be His joke for eternity. I will be remembered! I will be remembered!—if not in fame, then infamy."[3]

Considering it better to be famously hated than indifferently forgotten, Salieri decides to take responsibility for Mozart's death, falsely claiming to have murdered the beloved musician. As he describes it: "And now my last move. A false confession—short and convincing! For the rest of time whenever men say 'Mozart' with love, they will say 'Salieri' with loathing! . . . I am going to be immortal after all! And [God] is powerless to prevent it."[4]

So goes one story of lasting discontent. Antonio Salieri had achieved the most honored position in his field, accumulated great wealth, and frequently dined with the king. Mozart, on the other hand, had to teach private lessons to make ends meet and couldn't save enough money for a decent burial. So why was Salieri the one consumed with envy? How, despite such a comfortable and successful life, could he allow bitter jealousy to drive him insane?

We believe he may have had parents who mastered the second tactic for messing up a child's life: inspiring the deadly sin of envy.

Conventional Wisdom

Not surprisingly, conventional wisdom frowns upon the chief source of discontent, envy. It has even been given the unappealing label "the green-eyed monster." Of course, green is the shade one's skin turns when seriously ill and the color of unripe fruits that cause a stomachache. The image suggests sickness unto death caused by desiring something out of its proper season.

The "green-eyed" reference appears to have been coined by none other than William Shakespeare himself in his tale of self-destructive jealousy, *The Merchant of Venice*. "As doubtful thoughts, and rash-embraced despair, / And shuddering fear, and green-eyed jealousy!"[5]

But it is another Shakespeare play, *Othello*, that gives us a glimpse of the more troubling effects of a "green eye." Envious of the love between Othello and Desdemona, Iago tricks Othello into believing she has been unfaithful, driving Othello to murder his beloved in a fit of jealous rage. Thus, Iago succeeds in depriving Othello of that which he himself can't possess. Shakespeare reminds us of why envy is considered such an ugly vice. What it can't possess, it seeks to destroy.

Blinding Envy

In his letter to the church at Galatia, the apostle Paul listed "jealousy" and "envy" in a pretty nasty list of sins (Gal. 5:20–21). So did the apostle Peter, who commanded Christians to "rid [themselves]" (1 Pet. 2:1) of that which both men knew drove people to "hating one another" (Titus 3:3).

Another classic fable tells of two men standing before a wise king, each seeking a gift. One coveted and the other envied, driving each to hate the other. Aware of their bitter rivalry, the king promised to give each whatever he asked on one condition: "One of you must whisper your request in my ear while the other stays silent. I will grant the first one's request, but I will double it for the second to reward his restraint."

The first man was determined to receive twice as much as his competitor, so he kept his lips sealed.

The second thought to himself, *I refuse to let him walk away with more than me!* So he leaned toward the king and whispered, "My lord, I wish to have one of my eyes put out."[6]

Envy has long been seen as a "deadly" sin because, as with Salieri and the other two men, it can spawn attitudes and behaviors that drive us mad and make us blind.

What kind of blindness? Jesus told a story that offers a hint. He described a landowner who went out early one morning to hire men to work in his vineyard, agreeing to pay each a day's wage. Later that same day he needed more workers, so he hired several more. But this time he didn't specify how much he would pay, simply offering to pay "whatever is right" (Matt. 20:4). He did this again and again until the last hour of the workday when he hired the last few guys from the unemployment line.

Thanks to the landowner, everyone would earn a

paycheck that day. So, everyone should be happy, right? Wrong. Let's pick up the story as the final whistle blows.

> When evening came, the owner of the vineyard said to his foreman, "Call the workers and pay them their wages, beginning with the last ones hired and going on to the first." The workers who were hired about the eleventh hour came and each received a denarius. So when those came who were hired first, they expected to receive more. But each one of them also received a denarius. When they received it, they began to grumble against the landowner. "These men who were hired last worked only one hour," they said, "and you have made them equal to us who have borne the burden of the work and the heat of the day." (Matthew 20:8–12)

They had a point. After working a twelve-hour shift in the hot sun, they received the same pay as the guys who strolled in late in the day and worked a mere sixty minutes. If anyone had a reason to cry foul, it would seem these guys did: "Hey, what about us?"

The owner replied, "Friend, I am not being unfair to you. Didn't you agree to work for a denarius? Take your pay and go. I want to give the man who was hired last the same as I gave you. Don't I have the right to do what I want with my own money? Or are you envious because I am generous?" (Matt. 20:13–15).

Ouch! Good comeback. The workers and the land-owner had an agreement that was honored on both sides. The owner did nothing wrong, dishonest, or sneaky. He paid them 100 percent of the agreed-upon wage. So why all the complaining? In the words of the landowner, "Because I am generous."

The workers didn't gripe because they had it so bad, but because someone else had it better. We all tend to do that, blinding ourselves to our own blessings by glaring at the blessings of others. Someone else has the something we want: a nicer home, a newer car, a better job, a healthier body, a more attractive mate (or any mate at all). As a result, our green-eyed friend pokes his head up and shouts, "Hey, what about me?" We violate one of the Ten Commandments given to Moses on Mount Sinai: "You shall not covet your neighbor's house. You shall not covet your neighbor's wife, or his manservant or maidservant, his ox or donkey, or anything that belongs to your neighbor" (Exod. 20:17).

You might find it surprising that envy made God's top-ten list alongside such biggies as murder, theft, and adultery. At first glance the covet commandment seems out of place. After all, comparing and desiring what others have isn't like murder or theft. So why did God make such an issue of it?

Probably because covetousness warps our priorities. And when our priorities are wrong, our actions follow suit. God gave the caution against coveting such prominent billing precisely because it is such a natural part of our lives: a downhill tendency that has the potential of poisoning our whole existence. And the poison often spills over onto those around us.

Do you remember the 1994 Winter Olympics? The main media story focused upon two people competing in figure skating, Tonya Harding and Nancy Kerrigan. After a stranger clubbed Nancy Kerrigan in the leg, presumably to knock her out of the competition, Tonya's ex-husband was convicted of masterminding the attack and was sent to prison. Tonya was convicted of hindering an FBI investigation into the matter.

In the end, Nancy wound up with an Olympic medal and emerged as a national hero for overcoming a painful obstacle to obtain victory. Tonya, on the other hand, became a shameful reminder of what can happen when we feed petty jealousy and envy. And to think, every parent has the potential of raising the next Tonya Harding!

Artificial Poverty

Socrates called contentment "natural wealth," while labeling luxury "artificial poverty." He knew that the more stuff we can possess, the more we must possess.

And let's face it, most of our children live in relative wealth and prosperity. By historical standards, in fact, this generation of kids may be the most pampered in history. In the distant past, humanity struggled to acquire the basic provisions of life. Most people lived on farms, requiring long hours of hard work just to survive. But that was okay, because they expected no more.

And then one day, something happened. As I understand the story, a man named Sears came up with the idea of sending a catalog describing hundreds of wonderful products to every possible home on the prairie. Suddenly, without warning, the average American working his own farm was confronted with the things he didn't have: better tools for his work, new gadgets for his home, fancy clothes for his wife, and exciting toys for his children. Once the spectacular world of merchandise entered his home, the simple life was no longer enough. How could anyone be satisfied with basic provisions when so many other things were possible?

And so the process goes. Years later, just about the time most of us had acquired the things we wanted, something else happened. Another "catalog" hit our homes. It seemed harmless enough. The television, at first a novelty item, became the vehicle through which a whole new world of possibilities entered our homes. It brought us entertainment on demand, educated us about the world around us, and reminded us that life was not yet ideal. It convinced us that life should be more, much more.

In short, we discovered the secret to lasting discontent.

Mess-Up Strategies

Certainly there are some downsides to inspiring a strong sense of jealousy or envy in our children. But let's not overlook the potential benefits. Children who continually covet, for example, are more likely to view other kids as competitors to beat rather than playmates to enjoy. Anyone who has ever seen a child's beauty contest or league sporting tournament knows that moms and dads want their kids to compete and win, not relax and have fun!

We should also consider a child's long-term earning potential. We will deal with the specific benefits of greed later, but it should be noted that certain mess-up strategies nicely complement others and may even serve as necessary prerequisites. A content child could become a content adult who, in turn, could develop a diminished obsession with making money. Perish the thought!

So, let's explore a few strategies for helping inspire lasting discontent in our precious kiddos.

MESS-UP STRATEGY #1: CONTINUALLY COMPARE

It is much easier to instill discontent in children when they have a clear point of comparison. Obviously you'll want to avoid highlighting those who have less than your children. Put them in situations where others seem to have more, be more, do more, and enjoy more. Here are a few suggestions.

First, make a habit of driving through the really, really nice neighborhoods on your way to school, shopping, church, or just running errands. As you pass a house that is much bigger or better than your own, draw attention to it and ask your kids if they wouldn't prefer living in a great place like that. You might also want to subscribe to *Better Homes and Gardens*. Better than whose? Why, better than yours, of course!

Second, try to watch a lot of television shows that highlight the lifestyles of the rich, the famous, and the beautiful. You shouldn't have any trouble identifying at least one show per evening to enjoy envying together as a family. If you have a daughter, keep a special lookout for shows that celebrate women with tiny figures, since doing so can contribute to eating disorders and other patterns of self-loathing.

Third, window-shop until you drop! There are always new clothes, new toys, new movies, new household decorations, and new electronic gadgets to covet.

For really advanced training, make a point of comparing your children to "better" kids whenever possible. You'll want to comment on the natural athletic talent of some other kid on your child's soccer team or how smart the girl who won the spelling bee is. Be sure to make such comparisons in the presence of your kids, or much of the effect will be lost.

MESS-UP STRATEGY #2: DISCOURAGE GRATITUDE

It is impossible to be truly grateful and discontent at the same moment. When one begins listing his or her blessings and thanking God for the good gifts of life, dissatisfaction begins melting away like snow on a sunny day. That's why mess-up parents help kids avoid an attitude of gratitude.

Fortunately, this is one strategy that requires absolutely no effort. Gratitude is a habit that must be learned, not a natural tendency. Children who develop a pattern of thankfulness do so because a mom and/or a dad invested lots of energy teaching them to express appreciation at every turn. Mess-up parents, by contrast, leave kids to their own self-centered, demanding, ungrateful devices.

Don't expect little Susie to write a note of appreciation to her teacher or coach. Doing so can feed patterns that move her away from her natural bent toward entitlement. Remind her that she deserves whatever good things she gets, even more than other kids.

Never require Johnny to say "Thank you" after receiving a nice gift from Grandma or anyone else. How often have you been embarrassed by a child's impulse to grab and go rather than pause and appreciate? Don't be. Forget about sheepishly asking "What do you say?" in front of gift-givers anticipating thanks. Such questions force a discipline onto your kids that they don't want—and that could undermine their downhill momentum.

MESS-UP STRATEGY #3: MODEL RESENTMENT

Have you ever attended a ten- or twenty-year high school reunion? You'll see single women jealously eyeing the married-with-children gang. Proud blue-collar workers deflate while chatting with the white-collar crowd. Former cheerleaders who've gained thirty pounds politely hate former wallflowers who've lost twenty. The divorced single mom no longer hangs out with her former best friend who is now happily married to a successful architect. And nearly everyone leaves the event resenting those who seem to have a better lot in life.

Now, imagine mimicking that same experience every day in every way and you've got the basic concept. If you hope to mess up your children's lives, never let them catch you following the biblical admonition to "rejoice with those who rejoice" (Rom. 12:15). Instead, learn to "sorrow at another's good."[7] In short, model a spirit of resentment.

Let your kids hear you complain about your crummy

job and how someone else got the promotion that should have been yours.

Point out the unfairness when the neighbor gets a brand-new SUV while you still drive a dented mini-van, and demonstrate seething resentment.

You get the idea. Work hard to let your children hear you compare yourself to others. They need to learn that envy is not just about coveting something you want. It is about wishing others didn't have it either.

Taking Precautions

For those determined to mess up their children's lives by fostering the deadly sin of envy, increase your odds by ignoring the following suggestions designed to instill the opposing virtue of contentment.

> ### WARNING:
> *The following ideas could be hazardous to the process of messing up your child's life. Read at your own risk!*

NOT FAIR!

One of the ways we convince ourselves we have a right to be less responsible is by seeing life as unfair. When we get a bum rap, we excuse our own irresponsible attitudes and actions. Here is an activity to help undermine this tendency with your kids.

Bring the kids (ages seven to twelve) together and divide them into two teams. (The more kids the better, so do this activity when you have friends or relatives over to play. Even if the teams are two kids and two parents, however, it will work.) Tell the teams you wish to have a little contest between them. Starting with the older kids, give a time limit and offer some reward (a piece of candy, a quarter) for each successful hit with the plastic baseball bat or some other competitive task. The key to this activity will be making the time limit longer, the reward greater, and the task easier for the second team. When the first team wins eight quarters for hitting the baseball eight times in thirty seconds, they will be very happy. But when they see you giving a dollar for each successful hit in sixty seconds with easier pitches, they will immediately yell, "Not fair!"

This will provide an ideal opportunity to discuss Jesus' parable of the vineyard workers found in Matthew 20. Just like the workers in the parable, the first crew members thought they had a great deal until someone else got a better deal—then they thought they had a bum rap. This is like life. We are responsible to make the best of what God gives us without worrying or complaining or comparing to what others are given.

MOVIE NIGHT: *IT'S A WONDERFUL LIFE*

Since most of us watch this wonderful classic every Christmas season anyway, why not take a few moments to discuss the implicit message of George Bailey's life experience? After a lifetime of sacrificing his own dreams and ambitions for the sake of others, George encounters a crisis that pushes him to the end of himself. He envies the blessings of others, which causes him to become ungrateful for his own blessings. This causes him to sacrifice his own happiness and wish he had never been born. So the angel Clarence gives him what he asks for by showing George what life for others would have been like without him. In the end, George realizes just how wonderful life is—all thanks to a little change in perspective. Here are a few questions to draw out the key lessons of this film:

Question: Why did George wish he had never been born?

Answer: Because he was focused on his troubles and all the things he didn't get to do.

Question: What was so wonderful about George Bailey's life?

Answer: He helped a lot of other people.

Question: What is the message of this film?

Answer: That we have great worth, even if life doesn't turn out the way we expect.

Question: What Bible passage does the life of George Bailey model?

Answer: James 1:27.

FAMILY NIGHT ACTIVITY: AN ATTITUDE OF GRATITUDE

Fill a glass of water halfway and place it on the table in front of the children.

Give each child an index card with the phrase "The glass is half- _____" written on it and ask him or her to complete the phrase.

Once they've completed the phrase, go around and find out who wrote "full" and who wrote "empty" in the blank.

Now give each child a piece of drawing paper and crayons. Ask them to draw a large glass half-full of water. Ask them to spell the name or draw pictures of good things they already have (toys, books, family, food, clothes, etc.) in the portion of the picture *with* water.

In the space *without* water, have them write or draw things they would like to have, such as more money, a new toy, a vacation to Disneyland, a special kind of cereal, or whatever they can think of.

Read 1 Timothy 6:6–9 and Philippians 4:11–12 and discuss why it is important that we "learn" to be content no matter what we do or don't have. Then read Ephesians 5:20 and explain that the practice of expressing thanks is one way we make our lives "half-full" instead of "half-empty" because it helps us focus on the blessings God has given rather than complain about the things we don't have.

Wrap up your time by giving the children a stack of index cards and having them do a "Thanksgiving scavenger hunt" by running all over the house and identifying as many things for which they are thankful as they can in ten minutes (or as long as you like). Let them write a word or draw a picture to represent each blessing.

Gather back together and have the children pray a brief prayer of thanks for each card.

Memorize the jingle: *I'll be content with what God sent!*

CHAPTER THREE

Encouraging an Expressive Temper

(Deadly Sin: Anger)

The entire family sits together on the sofa consoling one another while passing a box of tissues. You would think someone would have warned them. Everyone must have assumed they already knew. But they didn't. So, like millions before them, this family popped what appeared to be a feel-good film into the DVD player with no idea just how it would end.

Of course, they had heard of *Old Yeller*, the classic Disney film based on the 1956 book by Fred Gipson. They had even heard the famous lyrics "Old Yeller— best doggone dog in the West!" They just didn't know the story. The cover seemed harmless enough, picturing an adolescent boy with his arm around a tongue-wagging dog in obvious affection for each other. What could be more "feel good" than a boy and his faithful canine?

Travis Coates, the boy, did indeed love Yeller. But not at first, when the dog kept stealing meat from their 1860 farmhouse. Travis's father had gone off to take the cattle to market, leaving the boy to watch out for his mother and kid brother. So you can imagine how irritated Travis became whenever provisions came up missing thanks to a thieving mutt. Hardly a good foundation for friendship.

All was forgiven, of course, after Yeller risked himself to save Travis's younger brother from an angry bear. The former enemies became best buddies, and the old dog became essential to life on the farm, including several more interventions that helped to protect the Coates family from harm.

So why all the sobbing on the sofa? Because something happens to Yeller that transforms the loving, gentle pet into an enraged animal that must be caged in order to protect the family from his fang-toothed rage. He contracts rabies while fending off a pack of ravenous wolves. The virus causes dogs to attack unprovoked, and a bite from a rabid animal can be fatal to humans. So it becomes necessary for someone to shoot Yeller in order to protect the family from harm as well as put him out of his misery. And, as "man of the house," Travis—Yeller's best friend and master—gets the job.

Please pass the tissues.

Rabies, a Latin word meaning "madness, rage, fury," conjures images of threatening dogs with foaming saliva and exposed fang teeth.[1] But unlike the trained guard dog eager to protect his master, a rabid pet will bite the hand that feeds it. In fact, those closest to the animal are most at risk because the germ incubates for a long period of time. The wound through which the virus spreads could heal long before the first unsuspecting victim is attacked.[2]

While in his right mind, Old Yeller protected Travis and his family from harm. When suffering the "madness, rage, and fury" of rabies, Yeller himself became a lethal menace.

Tempers Will Fly

Our youngest son plays hockey. We, of course, watch and cheer his games from the stands along with the rest of the hockey parents—which is where we discovered yet another aim for mess-up parenting. You see, tempers do fly in hockey arenas, and not just on the ice. So we wonder: does a causal connection exist among angry parents, hot tempers, and championship-level performance?

Case in point, the 2006 World Cup final game. French

team captain and soccer legend Zinedine Zidane demonstrated his own brand of madness, rage, and fury on the biggest athletic stage on the planet. Like many other athletes embroiled in the heat of battle, Zidane and Italian Marco Materazzi shared a not-so-pleasant verbal exchange. At first, Zidane walked away in a huff. But then, despite millions of television viewers across the globe watching his every move, he turned back toward the unsuspecting Materazzi, lowered his head like a big-horned ram, and proceeded to run full force into Marco's chest. Zidane was ejected from the game, but the head-butt made the highlights reel of every sports desk in the world and turned him, for some spectators, into a poster child for uncontrolled wrath.

Parents around the world watched in horror as an international sports legend threw a major temper tantrum with no serious consequences. You see, despite the attack, Zinedine Zidane was voted best player in that year's World Cup tournament. One must wonder, did Zidane's parents shout angry instructions from the sidelines when he played peewee soccer?

Tennis legend John McEnroe may be better remembered for his frequent tennis tantrums than his seven Grand Slam singles championship titles. Not only did McEnroe have a mean serve, he also had a mean streak that prompted him to throw rackets, pout off the court, and shout at the umpires. Nonetheless, McEnroe was inducted into the International Tennis Hall of Fame in 1999.

And who could forget the infamous Mike Tyson and Evander Holyfield 1997 championship fight? Tyson, who had already earned a reputation for angry outbursts, literally bit off a portion of Holyfield's ear. When they ended the fight over the clear violation, Tyson became furious, taking swings at anyone and everyone in his path. Hardly the picture of athletic professionalism, Mike Tyson later went to prison and filed for bankruptcy. But not before earning an estimated $300 million during a long and colorful boxing career.[3]

Zidane, McEnroe, and Tyson offer mess-up parents much-needed inspiration as we consider helping our own children discover the downhill potential of an expressive temper.

Conventional Wisdom

"Envy bites its nails," writes Henry Fairlie. "Wrath scratches and tears with them."[4] It head-butts. It throws rackets. It bites ears. In short, it becomes the "rabies" of anger, rage, and fury that infects us all.

Jesus said during his most famous sermon, "You have heard that it was said to the people long ago, 'Do not murder, and anyone who murders will be subject to judgment.' But I tell you that anyone who is angry with his brother will be subject to judgment" (Matt. 5:21–22).

Why on earth would the Lord compare being angry with one's brother to the heinous crime of murder?

Isn't anger a normal emotion that everyone experiences? Yes and no.

Anger is indeed an emotion, one that God Himself has been known to express. In fact, certain Scriptures list wrath as part of God's character:

- The wrath of God is being revealed from heaven against all the godlessness and wickedness of men who suppress the truth by their wickedness. (Romans 1:18)

- Because of these, the wrath of God is coming. (Colossians 3:6)

Other Scriptures unapologetically include anger among God's emotions:

- In furious anger and in great wrath the LORD uprooted them from their land. (Deuteronomy 29:28)

- Therefore the LORD's anger burns against his people; his hand is raised and he strikes them down. (Isaiah 5:25)

So, if God Himself deals with anger and wrath, why would Jesus take such a hard stand against it when found among mere mortals?

The problem, we are told, is not anger itself, but what we do with anger. Some things deserve our wrath. It would be wrong, for example, to passively yawn at child abuse. When we see a legitimate injustice, we should get mad. There is such a thing as righteous indignation.

Unfortunately, our anger is rarely in response to gross injustice. It is more typically tied to retaliation or tantrums.

Traditional Christian teachings recognize four levels of anger, only two of which would be labeled sinful. First, there is the simple emotion itself, neither good nor evil. Second, there is the emotion properly regulated so that it can be used to do justice or to correct what is wrong. The third category moves us into sin when the emotion oversteps appropriate application, usually out of a desire to punish another person who does not deserve such severe reaction. This is the sin we parents often fall into when we discipline in anger, sometimes because our children misbehaved in anger. Finally, and most sinful, is the stage when anger turns into hatred of another person, or even God Himself.[5]

As Peter Kreeft explains, "Getting angry at the wrong things, or getting too angry, is sinful; but getting rightfully angry, angry at the right things and to an appropriate degree, is not. The Psalmist implies this when he writes, 'Be angry, and sin not' (Ps. 4:4)."[6]

Aristotle put it like this: "Anyone can become angry, that is easy . . . but to be angry with the right person, to the right degree, at the right time, for the right purpose, and in the right way . . . this is not easy."[7]

Expert Opinions

So what do traditional parenting gurus say about children and anger? Not surprisingly, they want parents to discourage it, channel it, defuse it, or soothe it.

In his book *The Explosive Child*, for example, Dr. Ross Greene reminds parents that "the direct approach is usually not the ideal place to start" when it comes to confronting a child's explosive anger. As he explains, "Few of us learn best in an environment we experience as tense, hostile, and adversarial, and your child is no exception." That's why he recommends creating a "user friendly environment" that helps us adopt more realistic expectations about the kind and level of frustration the child can handle in order to better manage our own reactions and remain in the role of authority figures rather than combatants. Parents should learn how to respond to a child's reactions before he's at his worst to keep tempers from reaching the boiling point.[8]

Dr. Don Fleming offers helpful yet conventional advice in his book *How to Stop the Battle with Your Child*. In his view, parents should not take a child's angry outbursts personally because like it or not, we usually express anger at the people we feel safe with. So when you think your kid really has it in for you, he may also be telling you that he feels safe enough with you to let out some of his frustrations. So, instead of becoming emotional, implement a series of consequences. As Dr. Fleming describes:

> When your child continues with his angry reactions, you can respond in the following manner. "You still get too mad when I tell you to do something. . . . It's OK to tell me you're mad and that you don't always like to listen to me. But it's not acceptable for you to go on screaming and yelling at me. If you're unable to control this every time I ask you to do something, you will lose fifteen minutes of your playtime (or another consequence). If you still have trouble controlling yourself, the next time you act this way, it will be half an hour off playtime." . . . You are showing your child that you will be firm, will clarify what is expected of him, and will continue to work on his behavior until he learns to control himself.[9]

Dr. Dan Kindlon, co-author of the best seller *Raising Cain*, says, "If we don't give our kids enough time, understanding, attention, and love, they'll become chronically angry or depressed." As kids age, the research suggests, they need even more time with you, doing things such as sharing family dinners or enjoying a movie night routine. If they don't have this time, "they either pass on the pain they feel to others in the form of meanness or turn it against themselves in the form of depression."[10] In other words, plenty of uphill climbing is required of parents hoping to minimize their children's propensity toward the dark emotions.

Road Rage

You pull onto the freeway on-ramp in order to dart home after work on Friday evening, anticipating a hot meal and a relaxing bubble bath before reclining in your favorite chair to watch a great movie. But as you approach the interstate, you notice the painfully familiar glow of brake lights. Lots of brake lights. Looking down at your speedometer, you discover that you are moving at the blinding speed of nearly five miles per hour! That's right, for the fifth time in five days, you will spend the next two hours sitting in bumper-to-bumper traffic.

You know too well what this means. Your warm dinner will be sitting in the refrigerator covered with foil. Your bubble bath will downgrade to a quick shower. And the movie you wanted to rent will be checked out, so you'll just catch the evening news before drifting off to sleep.

No wonder so many urban commuters slip into a malady popularly called *road rage*. Anger rises to the point that otherwise kindhearted men and women find themselves saying bad words, beating the steering wheel, and aggressively cutting off other drivers without hesitation or regret. Wrath in response to injustice? Not really. More like fury in response to inconvenience.

An even more common form of road rage occurs nearly every week in our minivan. Our two youngest children share the third-row bench seat and have been known to suddenly slap, pinch, or punch each other. Our first clue typically comes in the form of an angry scream or a painful cry.

"What's going on back there?" one or both of us shout at the rearview mirror.

"He touched me!" or "She looked at me!" lets us know some serious offense will require parental intervention—sometimes accompanied by a bit of our own fury.

And so the cycle goes. One person interrupts the desires, needs, or space of another, which makes that person mad. That person retaliates to get even, and it escalates from there. Before you know it, you have an all-out feud between the Hatfields and the McCoys, the Crypts and the Bloods, the turn-signal users and the sudden lane swervers.

"A hot-tempered man stirs up dissension," wrote Solomon, "but a patient man calms a quarrel" (Prov. 15:18). Elsewhere he condemns a quick temper, saying that kind of anger "resides in the lap of fools" (Eccl. 7:9). No wonder unbridled wrath carries such a negative stigma.

God, by contrast, is described as "slow to anger" and full of forgiveness (Pss. 145:8; 86:5). And the Scriptures tell us that He calls us to do likewise: "Better a patient man than a warrior, a man who controls his temper than one who takes a city" (Prov. 16:32).

In his letter to the Colossians, the apostle Paul tells Christians to "rid yourselves" of things like anger and rage (Col. 3:8), just before he warns us not to "provoke" children toward wrath (Col. 3:21 KJV). Clearly, conventional wisdom considers anger a deadly sin and thinks moms and dads play a big part in feeding or starving the virus.

Mess-Up Strategies

It seems that anger, like the other deadly sins, builds upon itself and grows more intense and dramatic over time. A tiny oversight can bloat into a major source of bitterness. An accidental offense becomes an intentional vendetta. "He touched me!" is justification for "She pinched me!" and so on. That's what makes feeding a child's anger such an ideal way to mess up his or her life. Once the cycle begins, there is no saying where it might end.

How can mess-up parents encourage an expressive temper? How do we provoke our kids to wrath as part of our daily routines? We offer several suggestions.

MESS-UP STRATEGY #1: WALK ON EGGSHELLS

The best way to ensure that your child will develop an expressive temper is to create an environment of tension at home. Family members should learn to walk on eggshells around one another. If you know a child tends to throw toys or tantrums when he fails to get his way, by all means back off and give the kid what he wants. When your daughter insists on wearing socks that don't match to school and threatens to burst into a tearful fit of rage if forced to change them, apologize profusely for being such a mean parent. Such maneuvers reinforce the idea that expressing one's anger gets one's way.

Of course, you should expect of your children only what you are willing to model yourself. Children need to worry that Mom may lose her cool or Dad might blow his stack at any moment, creating an ongoing uneasiness that can breed insecurity and keep everyone on edge.

Olivia grew up in just such a family. Rather than a nurturing and forgiving environment, her home was filled with people at one another's throats. Every family has its occasional squabble, but hers rarely enjoyed peace and quiet. With no father around, Mom had four angry boys and two insecure daughters on her hands. Anger seethed and boiled on a daily basis. If you wanted to get your way, you yelled. If you were upset over someone else getting his way, you yelled. If you were exhausted and depressed over all of the yelling, you yelled. At any moment someone might explode in anger over the smallest issue, creating a never-ending cycle of rage and insecurity.

That is precisely the kind of environment sure to mess up a child's life by fostering a lasting resentment that, unless you walk on eggshells, can make them really mad.

MESS-UP STRATEGY #2: CORNER THEM

Have you ever seen a frightened, cornered cat or raccoon? He doesn't take very kindly to whoever happens to approach. Sensing no escape, the animal will likely arch his back and hiss a hateful sound before lashing out to attack. If, on the other hand, you back up to create a space through which he can scurry away, you will decrease the likelihood of attack. When the option exists, animals tend to take the path of least resistance.

One way mess-up parents encourage an expressive temper is by backing children into a corner. They shut down every legitimate avenue for expressing frustration or resolving real injustice. Feeling trapped, the children naturally lash out to attack.

Perhaps a more common way to visualize this strategy is to think of a bottle of carbonated soda. What happens when you shake the unopened bottle before twisting off the cap? At first glance, nothing much. In fact, as long as you avoid opening the drink, you might not realize your "offense" created any turmoil. But the moment you remove the cap, watch out for a major, sticky explosion! You need only one such experience to learn it is wise to gradually turn the lid and release some of the pressure when opening a shaken soda.

Every child feels anger from time to time, which is why conventional parenting experts encourage moms and dads to provide legitimate avenues for children to express and deal with frustration and process offenses. They suggest we provide a safe place for kids to let off steam within appropriate guidelines and to gently draw out their pent-up fizzles to prevent a major explosion. But such release valves can reduce the likelihood of a child realizing the full potential of his or her anger.

MESS-UP STRATEGY #3: LET THEM GET EVEN

When children feel they have been wronged, they will call for a chance to get even. Nothing could be more natural, or more helpful when trying to create a tense family environment. Allowing children to retaliate keeps anger rather than forgiveness in the driver's seat—and forgiveness is the one response capable of severely curtailing the cycle of revenge.

Jesus told His disciples to forgive over and over and over again. He knew that a soft answer turns away wrath. Revenge, on the other hand, invites ever more aggressive reactions. The kind of reactions that can reinforce a pattern of wrath.

When five-year-old Billy pushes four-year-old Bobby, pick up the lad and let him shove back.

If Sister One accidentally spills grape juice on Sister Two's favorite outfit, let Sister Two come up with a creative retaliation.

If another kid pokes fun at your son for being chubby, skinny, brainy, or slow, encourage him to pummel the brat. Countless bullies started out as insecure boys who just wanted to silence their critics.

We can feed the pattern of escalating anger by learning a lesson or two from the bullfighter. He uses a red cape to taunt, not pacify. He feeds the animal's fury. He doesn't quiet it. And no matter how angry the beast becomes, the matador never, ever backs off or retreats. In fact, the most exciting part of the match may be when the furious bull finally gorges the matador, getting even for his repeated offenses.

Let your children get even when offended or harmed. It will help them get ahead of the curve as they enter adulthood and must navigate the dog-eat-dog realities of the workplace, the rat race, and, of course, rush-hour traffic.

Taking Precautions

For those determined to mess up their children's lives by fostering the deadly sin of anger, increase your odds by ignoring the following suggestions intended to instill the virtue of self-control:

> **WARNING:**
> *The following ideas could be hazardous to the process of messing up your child's life. Read at your own risk!*

CAN'T TAKE IT BACK

There is toothpaste all over the plastic-covered table. Three young kids are having the time of their lives squeezing the paste out of their tubes, trying to expunge every drop the way Dad told them to.

"Okay," says Dad, slapping a twenty-dollar bill onto the table. "The first person to get the toothpaste back into their tube gets this money!" Little hands begin working to shove the peppermint pile back into rolled-up tubes—with very limited success. "We can't do it, Dad!" protests the youngest child.

"That is just like your tongue," he responds. "Once words come out of your mouth, it's impossible to get them back in. So be careful what you say in anger because you may wish you could take it back."

An unforgettable impression is made reinforcing the truth that we are responsible for what we say—for good or bad.

ENCOURAGEMENT FLOAT

Place an egg, a glass or jar of water, and a large bowl of salt before each of your children at the table. Tell them you are going to try to make the egg float in the water. First, place the egg in the water and tell everyone to yell at it. Say things trying to shame the egg into floating such as "Float, you dumb egg! Are you so lazy you can't even float to the top of the water?!" or "What are you, an egg or a mouse?"

Make the point that it is doing no good to get mad at the egg, so you're going to try encouragement. One at a time, each child is to stir spoonfuls of salt into the water while each person says one encouraging or complimentary thing about that child. Keep it up until the egg begins floating in the water. When each child has successfully floated his or her egg (and been encouraged), read Hebrews 10:24–25 together and discuss how treating others with respect and encouragement helps them do better, while angry disrespect and criticism cause them to sink. (Note: It takes a lot of salt to make this activity work, so be certain you have at least a cup on hand.)

MOVIE NIGHT: *GLORY*

For older teens, this powerful film is based upon the true story of the first black regiment in the Civil War. It features the experiences of several men who struggle to gain a sense of dignity after living as slaves and outcasts. One of the main characters in the story is an escaped slave named Trip (played by Denzel Washington), who blames everyone else for his misery. He picks fights, demeans those around him, and displays a generally sour attitude driven by his anger. In the end, however, he discovers with the other men in his regiment that self-respect and honor come to those who control their tempers and accept responsibility for doing what is right and honorable. Here are a few questions to draw out the key lessons of this film:

Question: Why was Trip such an unkind person throughout much of the movie?

Answer: He acted like a tough guy out of anger and misery.

Question: How did he eventually gain some self-respect?

Answer: By joining the others in doing what was right and honorable.

Question: What was the turning point for him?

Answer: When Sergeant Major Rawlins (played by Morgan Freeman) made him face how foolish he was being and encouraged him to join in the prayer-and-singing service around the campfire.

Question: Why would this have made a difference?
Answer: Because it helped him see the need to accept responsibility for changing his attitude.

Please note, this film has several disturbing battle scenes you might want to skip with younger children.

CHAPTER FOUR

Feeding a Voracious Appetite

(Deadly Sin: Gluttony)

In September 2006 an unprecedented decision shocked the world. Just as they were preparing to walk the runway in one of Europe's most prestigious fashion shows, 30 percent of the models scheduled to appear were disqualified from participation.

Certainly women had been eliminated from taking part in such events before, especially those who may have put on a few too many pounds. The elite of chic typically don't want chubby gals on the covers of their magazines or modeling the latest styles. This time, however, the girls were not turned away for being too fat. They were rejected for being too thin!

The show had become the target of protests from medical associations and women's advocacy groups because it tended to feature young ladies who were little more than skin and bones. So, according to news reports, the Madrid regional government decided to intervene, pressuring organizers to hire "fuller-figured women as role models for young girls obsessed with being thin and prone to starving themselves into sickness."[1]

During that same year the Robert Wood Johnson Foundation issued several reports on the growing epidemic of adult and childhood obesity in the United States. One report said the health "crisis" has been growing much worse over the past several decades. "Too many American adults and children are overweight or obese, and the trend is not getting any better."[2]

Sixty-seven percent of Americans are either obese or overweight, including 17 percent of kids six to nineteen years old. Over the past three decades, obesity among preschool-age children has more than doubled. Among those ages six to eleven, the rate of childhood obesity has more than tripled. The Johnson Foundation report tells us that the condition of being overweight or clinically obese leads to early development of hypertension, type 2 diabetes, and other life-threatening diseases.[3]

So, on one end of the scale we have models starving themselves to death, and on the other end we have children eating themselves into early graves. Might the two be connected? Could these trends be opposite sides of the same coin?

Yes, according to a 2007 study conducted by James Fowler, associate professor of political science at the University of California–San Diego. His research found that both obesity and thinness are "socially contagious." While genetics and metabolism certainly play a part in one's eventual weight, so do family and friends. The study published in a July 2007 issue of the *New England Journal of Medicine* reported a dramatic increase in the odds of an individual's becoming obese or slimming down when a close relative, friend, or loved one leads the way. The reason has much to do with what one's family and social network consider "acceptable norms" for weight.[4]

"Obesity tends to run in families," says Dr. Sandra Hassink, director of the Pediatric Weight Management Clinic. "Your child is much more likely to be obese if you or your spouse (or your youngster's grandparents) are overweight."[5]

No wonder kids who grow up with parents who overeat tend to join the party, and those who idolize twiglike supermodels often eat less than a healthy body requires. As the saying goes, the apple rarely falls very far from the tree.

Glorious Food

In one of their most delightful features to date, Pixar Animation Studios gave us a story that captures the good, bad, and ugly of our love affair with food. The main character of *Ratatouille* is a rat named Remy who happens to be a great chef. Unsatisfied with the garbage the rest of his family consumes, Remy craves the kind of variety, delicious smells, and endless combinations of flavors available in human kitchens. So he becomes the culinary brains behind a talent-challenged cook, and the two create many wonderful recipes on their way to rebuilding the reputation of a once-great restaurant in Paris.

Throughout the story, audiences enjoy relating to several characters who mirror ways each of us might interact with our food, beginning with the famous master chef, Auguste Gusteau. Gusteau, like his admiring disciple, Remy, has an almost romantic obsession with the form, aroma, and taste of a well-prepared dinner. He savors every moment, from gathering the ingredients in his kitchen to sampling the brewing soup to sipping the final drop of wine and swallowing the last bite of dessert at the end of a fine evening meal. A friendly, dramatic personality, Gusteau reflects supersized eating in his gigantic belly and second chin, lingering reminders of what certainly contributed to his early demise. But at least he enjoyed himself along the way.

On the skin-and-bones end of the scale is Anton Ego, the intimidating food critic who can make or break a restaurant with the stroke of his pen. Extremely selective about what he'll allow in his mouth, Anton remains as thin as a supermodel, complete with sunken eyes and emaciated face that match his nick-name, "the Grim Eater." Representing those who will eat only the best, Anton reveals in his dainty frame what might be considered an unhealthy aversion to the common dish—or the full portion.

Remy's brother Emile could be described as mod-estly overweight, but seriously unrefined. Like most of his rat friends and relatives, he eats anything and ev-erything without regard for the look, smell, or taste. In one scene, Remy expresses disgust when his brother eagerly eats a bit of trash without a clue what it is. Emile justifies his lack of taste, suggesting there are limitless food possibilities once you learn to "muscle your way past the gag reflex."

Pixar's delightful characters remind us of yet an-other way parents can mess up their children's lives: by introducing them to the wonderful and diverse world of a little obsession traditionally labeled *gluttony*.

Conventional Wisdom

The word comes from the Latin *gluttire*, which means "to swallow or gulp down." Common definitions include "overindulgence" and "overconsumption of food, drink, or other intoxicants to the point of waste."[6] In short, we swallow too much food or gulp down too much drink. And the results can be tragic.

Many of us know and love someone who has be-come addicted to alcohol or drugs, the most destructive forms of gluttony in every generation. Nothing is more heartbreaking than watching one's father, husband, mother, wife, or child fall prey to chemical addiction. By some estimates, 23 million Americans (nearly 10 percent of the population) have a drinking or drug problem serious enough to require professional treatment.[7]

But far more of us have fallen victim to gluttony tied to food. More than a third of us, 100 million Americans, would be described as obese or seriously overweight. Historically speaking, such a serious epidemic of gluttony is unprecedented. Most of human history has been characterized by a population struggling to eat enough, not gorging itself on too much. As *Time* magazine put it in a June 2007 feature explaining the physiological factors behind hunger, "Nature never planned for what could happen when unchecked appetites were suddenly matched by unchecked resources. But we're seeing it now."[8]

When modern ears hear the word *gluttony*, they tend to think of drunks, addicts, and overeaters. But its root reaches much further, touching those on both ends of the weight scale and all manner of self-indulgence. In order to understand why, we need to briefly look at the five categories of gluttony ancient and medieval Christians described.

1. HASTY (TOO FAST)

It is highly unlikely ancient church leaders sponsored many hot-dog-eating contests. The image of large men and women downing as many wieners as possible in sixty seconds just wouldn't fit their idea of Christian virtue. Nor would they appreciate drinking contests where one college student competes to finish off a bottle before another. Maybe that's why our grandparents told children to stop gulping their food.

2. EXPENSIVE (TOO RICH)

Remy the rat seems to represent this excess. He won't eat trash, which is commendable. But he also risks his life because he craves the rich, expensive foods found in the best French restaurants. Traditional Christian teachings would describe Remy's tendency as gluttonous because he invests too much of his time and energy thinking about and pursuing rich food and drink, ignoring Solomon's sage advice:

> When you sit to dine with a ruler,
>   note well what is before you,
> and put a knife to your throat
>   if you are given to gluttony.
> Do not crave his delicacies,
>   for that food is deceptive.

> Do not wear yourself out to get rich;
> have the wisdom to show restraint.
>
> (Proverbs 23:1–4)

3. EXCESSIVE (TOO MUCH)

Remy's hero, Chef Auguste Gusteau, portrays the excess typically associated with gluttony. His massive frame tells us he eats far more than sustenance requires. Another fictional character also comes to mind: Augustus Gloop from the film *Willy Wonka & the Chocolate Factory*. His insatiable appetite got him into serious trouble once he reached the factory and was unable to restrain himself when presented with the opportunity to eat and eat some more. Interestingly, he seems to have learned the pattern from parents who also enjoyed an extra serving or two. Traditional Christian teaching would point the entire family to the scriptural admonition: "Do not join those who drink too much wine or gorge themselves on meat, for drunkards and gluttons become poor" (Prov. 23:20–21). After all, as the research now shows, we are what those we hang around with eat.

4. GREEDY (TOO EAGER)

Bulimia is characterized by patterns of binging on massive quantities of food, then sticking a finger down your throat in order to purge. It serves as the modern-day equivalent of an ancient hedonism where it is rumored Roman citizens gorged themselves to the point of satiation before making a trip to the "vomitorium," then returning for a second round of gluttony.[9] Talk about "excessive consumption of food to the point of waste"!

Recalling this ancient practice, Christians in ancient times recognized that it is possible for us to cross a line where we lose the capacity to enjoy God's good gifts. Scratching and crawling our way over the divine design for healthy nourishment and flavorful refreshment, our greed drives one obsession—to consume the next mouthful. The Proverbs warn, "If you find honey, eat just enough—too much of it, and you will vomit" (Prov. 25:16). A glass of lukewarm water gives more pleasure and satisfaction to a thirsty man than a large chocolate milk shake gives a stuffed glutton.

Emile, the rat who pushed past the gag reflex so he could eat anything and everything, seems to embody this variation of the gluttonous spirit. He also pushes past the delicious blessing of appropriate moderation.

5. DAINTY (TOO PICKY)

The final and perhaps most surprising form of gluttony can be seen in the animated food critic, Anton Ego. He is driven by perfectionism. He will eat only food prepared just so. He would rather dwindle down to a thin rail than let anything touch his lips that isn't up to his self-determined standards of superiority. Anton considers himself a discerning connoisseur on a quest for excellence. Our great-grandparents would have called him a picky ingrate.

Some would place the epidemic growth of anorexia among young women in the "daintily" category of gluttony. While a complex disease, some believe it is motivated in part by the woman or girl's desire to achieve a self-defined standard of perfection. Of course, "perfection" usually means an unhealthy body image seen on magazine covers that drives girls to starve themselves.

Even among those who don't develop a life-threatening eating disorder, eating "daintily" (sometimes done by people known as *picky eaters*) can become a self-serving manipulation that falls squarely in the category of sin. It is unlikely ancient church fathers would have endorsed many modern diet fads, be it low carb, low fat, or any other variation that eliminates some of God's gifts instead of restraining much of man's appetite.

C. S. Lewis's demonic coach, Screwtape, explains this typically underappreciated category of self-indulgence in a letter to his apprentice on the art of temptation. After celebrating the fact that few churches ever preach on the topic of gluttony, he points to a very petite

Christian woman as an example of victory in this arena.

> She will be astonished . . . to learn that her whole life is enslaved to this kind of sensuality, which is quite concealed from her by the fact that the quantities involved are small. But what do quantities matter, provided we can use a human belly and palate to produce querulousness, impatience, uncharitableness, and self-concern?[10]

How does demanding an insufficient quantity or highly specific type of food ensnare one to gluttony? Screwtape explains, "Because what she wants is smaller and less costly than what has been set before her, she never recognizes as gluttony her determination to get what she wants, however troublesome it may be to others."[11]

Sounds like a few children we know. Maybe that's why our grandparents told their children to eat what's served or eat nothing at all.

A Bad Biblical Rap

A big part of conventional wisdom on the sin of gluttony comes from a large amount of biblical commentary on eating and drinking.

Solomon proclaimed "woe" on those who spend their entire day feasting, and "blessed" those who eat in a proper manner, "for strength and not for drunkenness" (Eccl. 10:16–17).

Jesus connected the anxieties of life and our tendency to become weighed down by "dissipation" and "drunkenness" (Luke 21:34). He certainly knew what drives us to the bottle or the binge.

The apostle Paul called drunkenness a "deed of darkness" and one of the ways we "gratify the desires of the sinful nature" (Rom. 13:12–14). He also described Christ's enemies, among other things, as people whose "god is their stomach" with destinies of "destruction" (Phil. 3:19). With such harsh biblical warnings, it's no wonder past generations considered gluttony such a serious problem.

On the positive side, the Scriptures also provide examples of what happens when we eat the right stuff in the right way. In the book of Daniel, for example, the conquering king of Babylon took the best and brightest young men from Israel into his court to groom them as servants. Right off the bat, these kosher Jews were offered the richest, daintiest foods at the king's own all-you-can-eat buffet and all the alcohol they could drink from his open bar. But in a move demonstrating tremendous willpower, Daniel asked permission for himself and his buddies to eat only the "salad bar" portion of the buffet: nourishing foods in healthy quantities. Unlike the other servants in training, Dan apparently had parents who taught him the dangers of gluttony.

To make a short story shorter, the Jewish boys turned out to be much stronger and keener than the rest due to their ability to control their appetites. Taking notice, the king promoted them above the guys standing in the dessert line.

Doctor Says

Not surprisingly, medical doctors have much to say on this subject. According to the American Academy of Pediatrics, parents with obese children tend to make several mistakes, starting with a counterproductive cycle of blame. They blame the kid, blame themselves, blame Great-grandma for handing down bad genes, and so on.[12] Not helpful. The blame game only keeps parents from exploring root causes of the problem in order to proactively manage rather than passively bemoan the situation.

A second common error is seeking the quick fix. Plenty of diet books and programs promise fast results, but obesity is not a problem that can be resolved quickly. Making matters worse, many of the more popular methods can be serious health hazards. That's why medical experts recommend working with a pediatrician and using plans based upon credible research.

Other parents do nothing to help their overweight children, naively hoping they will just "grow into" the excess pounds or waving off concerns because the entire family is "big-boned" and the poor kids need more food than most to "stay healthy."

On the other end of the spectrum are parents who allow their children to become overrun by a culture filled with pressures that "promote obesity but reward thinness." According to Dr. Dianne Neumark-Sztainer, who helped run the largest and most comprehensive studies of adolescent eating disorders ever conducted, "No wonder our teenagers are confused—at best—and dissatisfied with the way they look. At worst, they are suffering health-damaging excess weight, life-threatening eating disorders, or psychological pain that sends negative ripples through all aspects of their lives."[13]

Her advice? A list of goals for parents to develop in their adolescent kids, including:

- For the most part, accepting and celebrating their bodies.

- Nurturing and caring for their bodies with physical activity, healthy eating, and "avoiding unhealthy weight control and disordered eating habits."

- Maintaining body weights that are healthy for them while appreciating that different body shapes and sizes can be both healthy and beautiful.

• Rejecting "weightism" as unacceptable and refusing to fall victim to our culture's tendency toward "weight stigmatization."[14]

While every parent would agree that such aspirations are commendable, these goals also run counter to the general trends of society and basic human inclinations. In other words, they create an uphill climb!

Mess-Up Strategies

Mess-up parents acknowledge that Christian tradition views overconsumption and other food-related obsessions as sinful. But they do not lose heart because many cultures throughout history have actually celebrated the ability to indulge as a status symbol tied to wealth. Only those who can afford plenty of food overeat. Only those with the income to buy the best can be picky. And supermodels set the standard for the daughters of the first-world rich, not the third-world poor. So, while there are certainly risks to living in a self-indulgent culture, it can't be all bad. Let's face it, cookbooks and diet guides dramatically outsell the writings of ancient religious mystics!

That's why we think it is helpful to focus on strategies for embracing and perpetuating the old-school thinking called *gluttony* to help our kids develop patterns that will enable them to go with the flow of self-indulgence rather than fight the never-ending battle of self-discipline.

MESS-UP STRATEGY #1: MODEL INDULGENCE

Since children tend to adopt the patterns and pounds of their loved ones, mess-up parents try to model indulgence. They find a culinary passion and throw themselves into its mastery. They exceed recommended quantities of alcohol so the kids can see first-hand the joys of intoxication. They spend lavishly on expensive foods in large quantities and spend all their waking moments anticipating the next tasty entrée or glass of wine to demonstrate the kind of slavish compulsion a life of gluttony can become. And the best part is that these parents get to enjoy every bite, every sip, and every gulp, all while modeling important life attitudes for their children to mimic.

MESS-UP STRATEGY #2: TRAIN THEIR PALATES

We are all creatures of habit. And we are never more susceptible to acquiring tastes, developing patterns, and establishing habits than when we are young. The reason you can't teach an old dog new tricks is because it is stuck on those it mastered as a pup. So parents who want to mess up a child's life when it comes to food and drink need to train his or her palate to crave things that contain the most taste with the fewest possible nutrients. And that's the good news, because we live in a society that makes doing so very easy.

We may just be the first society in history where the rich tend to be thin while the poor tend to be plump. Compare the price of junk food to the price of healthy stuff on your next trip to the grocery store, and you'll discover why the closer one lives to the poverty line, the further you get from a thin waistline. That's because it is cheap and easy to buy sugary, fatty, processed foods. It requires much more work and money to prepare healthy meals with fresh, wholesome ingredients. The easy route, in other words, is to save money by training your kids to eat poorly. A few suggestions . . .

Fast food. We parents are constantly running from soccer practice to school events to the mall to music lessons and a hundred other routine carpool jaunts. We've all discovered how many of the popular fast-food chains offer "value menus" where for a few bucks we can buy the kids a fat-infested burger, a delicious pile of greasy fries, and two deep-fried apple pie desserts. This ease of ordering is very considerate of the restaurants, since it is much faster and cheaper to zip in and out of the drive-through window than to stop off at the grocery store to buy fresh strawberries, grapes, or whole wheat crackers. Of course, we could throw a cooler with healthy snacks in the car. But thanks to fast-food chains, we need not worry ourselves over such matters. We can just drive through!

Sugary cereal. Past generations recognized breakfast as the most important meal of the day, so then parents insisted upon a balance of protein, fat, fruits, and carbohydrates to start the day out right. Oatmeal, juice, and toast did the trick. But times have changed. Our grandparents didn't contend with countless television ads telling kids about the many great-tasting sugary cereals. Nor did they have the opportunity to stock up with a "ten boxes for ten bucks" deal at the grocery store. We, on the other hand, have the opportunity to give our children very little nourishment for mere pennies per day!

Soda and snack drinks. Do you remember all the effort required when we were little to get a glass of Kool-Aid? Mom had to tear open a package, scoop out the right amount of sugar, fill the pitcher with cold water, and then stir the mixture just to create a quart of liquid refreshment. No wonder she told us to just drink water when thirsty. She didn't want the hassle.

Today we can pick up a large box of canned soda or prepackaged drinks for kids to guzzle at home, take to school, share with soccer teammates, or sip in the car. Not only do these drinks require no effort for the parent to mix and serve, each package comes complete with its own plastic straw! How much more convenient could it be to help our children develop a taste for sugary drinks instead of bland, healthy water?

We could go on. Suffice it to say that training your child's palate for gluttony is nowhere near as hard as it used to be.

MESS-UP STRATEGY #3: GIVE THEM WHAT THEY WANT

Last but not least, be sure to adopt a "Just give them what they want" mind-set when it comes to diet. We need to move past the bias that sees children as incapable of making their own choices about what they'll eat or not eat, drink or not drink.

If your son likes double-stuffed Oreo cookies, keep a large supply on hand so he never has to go without.

If your little girl "needs" a large bowl of Froot Loops before bed in order to prevent midnight hunger pangs, pull out the bowl and spoon!

If your teenage boy is interested in having a few beers with buddies while out on the lake, buy him the good stuff.

If your adolescent daughter wants to drink a light Frappuccino in place of dinner so that she can look like the latest pop star, don't worry about it. Take her word for it when she says she is still full from the carrot stick she ate for lunch.

And if your child asks for a pass from gym class because he or she gets easily winded during dodgeball, by all means rescue the kid from such embarrassment.

Again, the key is putting the child in charge of his or her own choices in such matters. What better way to help your child perceive you as a loving mom or dad?

Taking Precautions

For those determined to mess up their children's lives by fostering the deadly sin of gluttony, increase your odds by ignoring the following suggestions designed to instill the virtue of temperance.

> **WARNING:**
> *The following ideas could be hazardous to*
> *the process of messing up your child's life.*
> *Read at your own risk!*

TURKISH DELIGHT

There is a scene in C. S. Lewis's *The Lion, the Witch and the Wardrobe* that is both central to the story and helpful for parents in discussing the sin of gluttony with their children. Edmund is presented with an enchanted box of his favorite tasty treat, Turkish Delight. The White Witch offers Edmund as much as he wishes if he will deliver his brother and sisters to her. While under normal circumstances Edmund would not have betrayed his siblings, a ravenous desire for more Turkish Delight overtakes his better judgment and he agrees. As the rest of the story unfolds, Edmund learns that his sin places his siblings, the good people of Narnia, and himself in grave danger, requiring the sacrifice of another to overcome choices made because he was unwilling or unable to curtail his appetite. After reading the book, listening to the audio drama, or watching the film version of the story, discuss the dangers of gluttony with your children, emphasizing the poor choices made when we allow appetite rather than good sense to rule our lives.

MOVIE NIGHT: *SUPER SIZE ME*

If you really want to alert your children to the dangers of gluttony, rent a copy of the documentary *Super Size Me* by Morgan Spurlock. It chronicles the story of a healthy, trim man who decides to go on a monthlong diet of nothing but fatty fast food. While the specific target of the documentary is McDonald's, the themes extend far beyond by showing what happens to us when we throw off balance and restraint, as well as how quickly poor dietary choices can impact our health and well-being. Because there are some disturbing and occasionally offensive elements to the film, be sure to preview it yourself first and skip the sections inappropriate for child viewing.

PANTRY INVENTORY

Create a family activity in which you all look through the pantry together in order to inventory which items should be classified as healthy and which belong in the junk-food pile. You may find that junk occupies a larger percentage of your family's grab-a-bite options than it ought to. After conducting the inventory, head off to the grocery store together and discover the wide range of healthy eating options available to bring balance to your pantry's scale.

HUNGRY HIPPOS

There is a famous Hasbro board game called *Hungry Hungry Hippos* available in the game section of most large department stores, such as Walmart or Target. Build a family night around the game by playing round after round, pausing in between to read the following Scriptures and briefly discussing the dangers of gluttony: Proverbs 23:2, 21; Daniel 1:8–16.

After playing the game, reading, and discussing,

memorize this together: *Glutton hippo eats it all, but we can choose not to fall.*

Give everyone permission to use the phrase with one another (within the family only!) whenever someone is behaving in ways that reflect a spirit of gluttony to remind him or her to avoid falling too far downhill.

CHAPTER FIVE

Discouraging
Frivolous Generosity

(Deadly Sin: Greed)

Bud Fox grew up in a blue-collar neighborhood where neither his folks nor his friends knew the meaning of the word *pretentious*, let alone displayed any of its traits. They were hardworking, middle-class people who loved their families and shared with the less fortunate. They considered a man's word his bond and a handshake more valuable than any legal contract. Bud grew up knowing the meaning of the word *integrity* because his dad organized its fan club.

But like many young men of modest means, Bud wanted more than the kind of provincial life his upbringing offered. So, thanks to Dad's overtime and scrimping to pay tuition bills, Bud pursued his dream of becoming a stockbroker in New York City, the global capital of cash and commerce. And before he knew it, Bud found himself being tutored by one of the most aggressive and successful financial wizards around—a man described as having had "an ethical bypass at birth" who opened Bud's eyes to an entirely different code of ethics than the one his blue-collar father modeled.

In a now infamous speech delivered before nervous corporate managers and stockholders, Bud's money-magnet mentor said three words that would radically change everything for the ambitious young apprentice: "Greed is good."

Watching Gordon Gekko (played by Michael Douglas) present his case in the 1987 film *Wall Street* is a study in the art of persuasion. As handsome as he was charming, Gekko wins over the initially skeptical crowd by inviting them to embrace a "survival of the fittest" ethic.

"Greed is right," he explains. "Greed works. Greed clarifies, cuts through, and captures the essence of the evolutionary spirit. And greed, in all of its forms . . . has marked the upward surge of mankind."

Gekko persuades the crowd of investors to support his takeover plan by appealing to a universally tempting "virtue." He also waters Bud's seed of ambition, nurturing what becomes an all-consuming obsession to have more, be more, earn more, and, if necessary, take more.

Bud's father clearly disapproves of his son's new value system, which the younger dismisses as the jealousy of a machinist "who can't stand that his son has become more successful than he has."

His hurt dad responds in anger: "What you see is a guy who never measured a man's success by the size of his wallet!"

Those who've seen the movie know that Bud runs into trouble after embracing that philosophy and following Gekko's example of "the end justifies the sometimes illegal and unethical means." But not before demonstrating the motivating influence of a five-letter seed buried deep within every child's heart, just waiting to be watered by Mom or Dad Gekko—the seed called *greed*.

Kids Say . . .

The darndest things come out of the mouths of children, often reflecting what might have gone into their ears at home. Seven-year-old Tim clearly understands what counts in life if his conversation with his buddy Mark is any sign. Mark's mom, a participant in the conversation, recaps the discussion as follows:

> TIM: I want to buy me an airplane.
> MARK'S MOM: Airplanes cost a lot of money.
> TIM: I know, but I'm saving up for it.

MARK: I could give you my allowance to help you save up.

MARK'S MOM: It would take a while to save that much even with your allowance, Mark, because a plane costs even more than a house.

TIM (IN A BOASTFUL TONE): Not my house. My house would sell for $580,000!

Tim didn't exactly pound his chest, but he did betray a hint of market value snobbery. And where, we must ask, does a child learn to boast about the value of his home? Perhaps from a mom and a dad who have made it a priority to instill the important life lesson that *greed* (and the bragging rights that come with it) *is good*.

Conventional Wisdom

Of course, conventional wisdom does not consider greed a virtue. In fact, greed finds itself on the list of deadly sins, sometimes wearing the alternate label *avarice*, which means "to crave."[1]

One prayer book defines greed as "too great a desire for money or worldly goods."[2] Greed is said to come in a variety of forms and colors, equally present in the stingy and the extravagant, the hoarding spendthrift and the charging shopaholic, the tightwad saver and the high-rolling gambler. Those who buy everything in sight and those who protect their pennies under lock and key betray the same root: *vice*. So do those who, like Gordon Gekko, view earning more the highest good—even if other goods must be sacrificed along the way.

Parents who want their children to pursue one or more variations on the vice of greed might find it helpful to know some of the bad press it received in the past.

The Golden Touch

Do you remember the Greek fable of a king named Midas? He possessed more gold than anyone in the world, yet he was not satisfied. He became obsessed with the acquisition of more and more and was happiest when he entered the palace vault to count what he possessed. The only thing he loved more than gold was his young daughter, Marygold.

One day, King Midas encountered a mysterious stranger who gave him the power to turn everything he touched into gold. Accepting the gift, he eagerly ran through the palace, transforming one object after another into gold.

He encountered a few problems, like the time he decided to read a book. When he touched the edge of the cover, the book became a block of gold. "I can't read now," he said, "but it is still much better to have a gold book than a book I can read."

When breakfast arrived, Midas reached for a piece of

fresh fruit. Upon picking up the fruit, however, it became a fruit-shaped lump of gold. The same happened to his glass of water. "What shall I do?" he asked. "I am hungry and thirsty yet cannot eat or drink."

Just then Marygold came into the room with tears streaming down her cheeks. She reached out for a comforting embrace from her father, and he instinctively kissed her. To his horror, she suddenly turned to gold. She had changed from a loving, happy little girl to a solid, golden little statue. King Midas screamed in anguish as he realized what he had done to the person he loved more than life itself.

Suddenly, the stranger reappeared. "Are you happy, King Midas?" he asked.

"How could I be happy?" replied the king. "I am the most miserable man alive."

"But you have the golden touch," said the stranger. "What more could you want?"

King Midas was silent a moment in his shame. "Please," pleaded the king, "give me back my precious Marygold, and I will give up all the gold I have! I have lost all that is worth having."

"You are wiser than you were," said the stranger. After instructing the king on how to reverse his golden touch, the stranger once again vanished.[3]

As King Midas learned the hard way, the most important things in life can be lost—not the least of which is happiness itself—as a direct consequence of greed.

Miserly Misery

Perhaps the most common image that comes to mind when we think of the greedy is the miserly—someone who bolts the vault door behind him so he can indulge himself in what he considers life's greatest pleasure: recounting his money, tenderly caressing each coin, and tidily stacking all the cash. The image reminds us why the word *miser* comes from the same Latin root as "misery"[4]—perhaps because, according to the Scriptures, misery is precisely the rent avarice charges its tenants.

- A stingy man is eager to get rich and is unaware that poverty awaits him. (Proverbs 28:22)

- A greedy man stirs up dissension, but he who trusts in the LORD will prosper. (Proverbs 28:25)

The Scriptures also warn that a wealthy, materialistic culture can breed loss of faith in God. Consider the warning the people of Israel received as they entered the promised land:

> Be careful that you do not forget the LORD your God. . . . Otherwise, when you eat and are satisfied, when you build fine houses and settle down, and when your herds and flocks

> grow large and your silver and gold increase
> and all you have is multiplied, then your
> heart will become proud and you will forget
> the LORD your God. (Deuteronomy 8:11–14)

Children growing up in modern-day America are without question the most at-risk group in history in this regard. Perhaps that is part of the reason more than half of those who grow up attending a Christian church abandon it by the time they graduate from high school.[5]

The most pervasive bad press on avarice comes from the stories told in every generation portraying the self-centered and self-protective as rather unattractive characters. Take, for example, the story Jesus told in response to the question: "Who is my neighbor?" In the parable of the good Samaritan, the Lord described what happened when a man was robbed, beaten, and left for dead on the side of the road. Two religious leaders, a priest and a Levite, saw the man. But instead of stopping to help, each "passed by on the other side" of the road (Luke 10:31). In other words, they ignored the needs around them and minded their own business. We don't admire their behavior, nor are we intended to.

The Samaritan, on the other hand, is a guy everyone likes. After all, he went out of his way to care for the injured man, even going so far as to spend his own money to put the man up in a swanky hotel and hire a caring nurse. Generosity wins the day while the misers fade away in their solitary habits of spreading misery.

One of the most severely condemned manifestations of avarice in the Christian tradition is a hard heart toward the poor, both in refusing to give to those in need or impatiently demanding debt repayment. Both of these unattractive tendencies are personified in a famous fictional character created by Charles Dickens, motivated by his own childhood experience of living with the shame and indignity of poverty as wealthy elites walked on the other side of the road.

We won't bother retelling the entire tale. You remember its four ghostly visitations to a Christmas-loathing humbug named Ebenezer Scrooge—whom Dickens describes as a "squeezing, wrenching, grasping, scraping, clutching, covetous, old sinner." And how the Scrooge everyone fears and despises gets transformed into "as good a friend, as good a master, and as good a man, as the good old city knew, or any other good old city, town, or borough, in the good old world."[6] In short, the novella paints a portrait of both greed, Scrooge One, and generosity, Scrooge Two.

Scrooge One is a man who, if possible, seems happy in his misery (or at least content there) and unconcerned that he emanates the darkness of hell even as those around him bask in the light of heaven. Wealth fails to warm his spirit, as surely as poverty fails to chill theirs. Dickens paints him as a man possessing all the qualities necessary to repel rather than invite human affection.

> Hard and sharp as flint, from which no steel had ever struck out generous fire; secret, and self-contained, and solitary as an oyster. The cold within him froze his old features, nipped his pointed nose, shrivelled his cheek, stiffened his gait; made his eyes red, his thin lips blue; and spoke out shrewdly in his grating voice. A frosty rime was on his head, and on his eyebrows, and his wiry chin. He carried his low temperature always about him; he iced his office in the dog days; and didn't thaw it one degree at Christmas.[7]

His cold, prickly shell served its purpose. None stopped to greet him on the street. Beggars knew better than to seek his charity. No children asked him the time. "Even the blind men's dogs appeared to know him," says Dickens, "and when they saw him coming on, would tug their owners into doorways and up courts; and then would wag their tails as though they said, 'No eye at all is better than an evil eye, dark master!' "[8]

Scrooge One is the kind of person none of us want to know but all do know. In fact, at certain times and in certain ways, he is someone we all can be. We all hide from those reflecting the warm light of heaven whenever we imprison ourselves in the cold, dark solitude of selfishness and greed.

Eyes accustomed to darkness abhor bright light. Dark hearts do the same. But in Scrooge's case, the warm glow he guarded himself against finally invaded his pale existence. The crooked wick of Ebenezer's candle finally gets lit.

And what a lighting! Literally overnight, a hard, miserly Mr. Scrooge becomes the lovable, generous Uncle Ebenezer. After dragging the reader through the journey of Scrooge One in 95 percent of the story, Dickens finally makes it all worthwhile by introducing Scrooge Two. It doesn't take long. We get only a few snapshots of what can happen when light overtakes darkness, such as when Scrooge turns a sled-pulling child into coconspirator by sending the prize turkey to Bob Cratchit's home. "Go and buy it, and tell 'em to bring it here, that I may give them the direction where to take it. Come back with the man, and I'll give you a shilling. Come back with him in less than five minutes and I'll give you half-a-crown!"[9]

Or when he shocks the skeptical charity director by making a sizable donation to the poor: "Not a farthing less. A great many back-payments are included in it, I assure you."[10]

Or when he playfully scares his tardy employee at work the following morning:

I am not going to stand this sort of thing any longer. And therefore, I am about to raise your salary! I'll raise your salary, and endeavor to assist your struggling family, and we will discuss your affairs this very afternoon, over a Christmas bowl of smoking bishop, Bob! Make up the fires, and buy another coal-scuttle before you dot another I, Bob Cratchit![11]

It is no accident that each of the snapshots illustrating Ebenezer's redemption shows him performing some act of generosity. He transforms from a self-centered miser into a charitable neighbor; from one who walks on the other side of the road to a good Samaritan. Dickens knew something parents who want to mess up their children's lives must recognize: giving is the antidote to hoarding, and generosity unlocks the shackles of avarice.

Greed's Antidote

Traditionally speaking, avarice is not merely the love of possessions. It is the love of *possessing*. It is fine for us to desire material things as a means to better living. But the greedy view money and things not as means, but as ends. The goal is to own more and more so that, well, we can own more and more. Things move from icons of God's goodness to idols of our own god delusion. As Henry Fairlie says, greed "leads to a form of self-annihilation" because people "become their possessions, who do not possess but are possessed by them."[12]

The pyramid tombs of ancient Egypt come to mind. Deciding maybe you can "take it with you," kings ordered vast treasures delivered to the grave along with their mummified bodies, which were placed in opulent, gold-laced caskets. In some cases, loyal servants were ordered to remain in the tomb with their deceased rulers—buried alive as other "possessions" the king wanted on display in his hall of fame. In his god delusion, the king believed he had assembled an everlasting tribute to himself—an idol of his own greatness. But in truth, his body faded into a gruesome corpse, and his memory vanished as a vapor of history. The stuff remains as a testimony to that which defined his existence.

Something similar happens to all of us. We don't erect vast memorial tombs, but we do display our designer labels, count our cash reserves, and brag about our property values, all in an effort to assemble some sense of identity in a culture consumed by material possessions and monetary growth. In the process, we diminish ourselves from people created in the image of God to people defined by the images of our stuff.

Contrast Scrooge One and Scrooge Two and you are reminded of several biblical admonitions:

- Command those who are rich in this present world not to be arrogant nor to put their hope in wealth, which is so uncertain, but to put their hope in God, who richly provides us with everything for our enjoyment. Command them to do good, to be rich in good deeds, and to be generous and willing to share. In this way they will lay up treasure for themselves as a firm foundation for the coming age, so that they may take hold of the life that is truly life. (1 Timothy 6:17–19)

- Remember this: Whoever sows sparingly will also reap sparingly, and whoever sows generously will also reap generously. Each man should give what he has decided in his heart to give, not reluctantly or under compulsion, for God loves a cheerful giver. . . . This service that you perform is not only supplying the needs of God's people but is also overflowing in many expressions of thanks to God. (2 Corinthians 9:6–7, 12)

- He who gives to the poor will lack nothing, but he who closes his eyes to them receives many curses. (Proverbs 28:27)

- We must help the weak, remembering the words the Lord Jesus himself said: It is more blessed to give than to receive. (Acts 20:35)

As we've touched upon in other chapters, Christian tradition offers an antidote to every vice, a means of inoculating ourselves against becoming invested by the kind of sickly life each deadly sin can spread. In the case of greed, the antidote is generosity. Nothing undermines finding your identity in stuff like giving it away. That's probably why our Lord told the rich young ruler that he needed to sell everything and give it to the poor if he wanted to find eternal life. Jesus wasn't describing an alternative path to heaven but inviting the young man to free himself from the hell on earth we experience when in bondage to greed; release from the misery of the miserly.

Mess-Up Strategies

Every act of charity acts like a dose of pink antibiotic medicine attacking a child's infection. Twice a day for ten days, and the cough is gone. Those who allow their children to become generous with others risk having the same thing happen to greed. That's why mess-up parents focus on discouraging frivolous generosity. Here are some of the more effective strategies to do just that.

MESS-UP STRATEGY #1: FOCUS ON STUFF

The single most important thing parents can do to help their children develop a strong sense of greed is to immerse them in a culture of stuff. Talk about the things you own, wish to own, and could own if you struck the lottery. Spoil them silly with the best brands, the latest electronic gadgets, the most expensive athletic shoes, and enough pocket cash to buy themselves and their friends a chocolate milk shake whenever they feel inclined.

And whatever you do, don't make them earn the money or things—that will only cause them to connect the dots between value and effort, which can seriously undermine the kind of entitlement attitude vital to a materialistic adult. Your kids should be given what they want because they want it, not because they've worked for it.

And not just any old stuff will suffice. Messed-up kids grow up expecting to have the finest things. Just imagine the humiliation of being caught wearing last year's hot brand on this year's opening day of school! Or worse, discovering that every other kid owns the latest electronic gadget while you're stuck with the one you got last Christmas. Learning to live without things instills character in children. And character is the last thing a messed-up child needs because it discourages him or her from developing an identity based upon stuff.

MESS-UP STRATEGY #2: CRITICIZE THE POOR

Have you ever been confronted with an opportunity to give to the needy in front of your children? Perhaps you've encountered a teenager selling magazines as a fund-raiser for underprivileged youth, or a mother and child holding a "Will work for food" sign on the side of the road, or an offering plate in church during Christmas Eve services to help the benevolent fund. Such situations provide an ideal opportunity to instill a callous, judgmental attitude in your child about those in need. After resisting the urge to donate, use some variation of the following to justify your refusal:

- In a country like this, people should be able to pull themselves up by their own bootstraps. Giving a handout only hurts them by taking away their motivation to work.

- I gave at the office.

- I never give anything to beggars because they deserve what they get since they are probably drunks.

And of course, the most famous line of all:

- Are there no prisons? Are there no work houses? Those who are badly off should go there![13]

MESS-UP STRATEGY #3: FORBID SACRIFICIAL GIVING

If your children must give to something, forbid them to give too much. A child's sacrificial giving out of compassion is very dangerous when you're trying to create a greedy child. So, in those situations when giving is inevitable, teach the kids how to use charity as a means of personal benefit.

The scene from the 2001 movie *I Am Sam* comes to mind. A hotshot lawyer (played by Michelle Pfeiffer) finds herself meeting with a mentally disabled man named Sam (played by Sean Penn). His precious daughter has been taken away by social services. At the mercy of a system dead-set against Sam and his daughter reuniting, he visits the lawyer to ask for help. Of course, there is no money to pay her, and she is in no mood to take a charity case. So she shoos Sam out of her office, hoping to get rid of the problem. But Sam returns, this time asking for help in front of her colleagues. Seeing an opportunity to improve a not-so-positive image, the lawyer announces that she had intended to accept the case all along. If she must give, she might as well earn some points along the way.

Mess-up parents model such tactics and help kids discover smaller variations on the same theme. For example, encourage them to share with the popular kids in order to win friends and influence people. Or hand them a twenty-dollar bill as the church offering basket passes, making a large, sweeping motion with your arm to make sure those around see just how generous your child is about to be. If confronted with a panhandler who won't go away, hand him a buck and explain to your child, "It was the only way to get rid of him."

If your child is anything like young Mark, who, as we described at the start of this chapter, demonstrated a willingness to give his allowance to a friend—be sure to forbid such acts of sacrifice. After all, nobody wants his or her child to become the next Mother Teresa!

Taking Precautions

For those determined to mess up their children's lives by fostering the deadly sin of greed, increase your odds by ignoring the following suggestions designed to instill the virtue of generosity.

> ### WARNING:
> *The following ideas could be hazardous to the process of messing up your child's life. Read at your own risk!*

A TWO-LETTER WORD

There is a word that every child dreads, but that every parent needs to learn. It is a simple, two-letter word that can make the difference between kids who are spoiled and ill-equipped for real life and kids who have learned that the world will not jump at their beck and call. It is the word *No*. During the early years, children need to hear it periodically from Mom and Dad. Not always. Not harshly. But they do need to learn from us that they cannot have everything they want.

It will happen as you pass the grocery store aisle with the colorful box of sugar-filled cereal with a special offer inside. The kids will ask, then plead, then beg, then demand that you get it for them. Say no and stick to your guns. It will happen as you are standing in line waiting to pay too much for too few items and they spot the candy bar display. They will whine, throw tantrums, and embarrass the living daylights out of you. Say no and make them regret making a scene when you get home.

Parents who can't say no to their younger kids face the potential heartache of grown kids who believe the world should give them what they want, when they want it. So start your kids on the right path. Let them hear that powerful little word now and then: *No*.

ROLLING IN MONEY

Kids have a hard time understanding the value of money. One day, Kurt went to the bank and withdrew one thousand one-dollar bills from our savings account. (Yes, they gave him funny looks.) He very carefully took the pile of money home and created a large money stack hidden behind some large boxes in the play area. We blindfolded the children and led them into the room, removed the blindfolds, and told the kids to find the secret treasure. After looking around, they finally found the cash pile—and promptly went nuts! "We're rich! We're rich!" they shouted while throwing money in the air and rolling in cash.

We instructed the kids to count the cash to let us know how much we had. Deep within the pile, I placed an envelope labeled "Special Stewardship Instruction" for the kids to discover. The envelope contained three Bible passages with instructions on how to use the money. The kids were told they could spend everything that remained after we met our stewardship requirements:

- Malachi 3:10—Give 10 percent to God.

- Proverbs 30:24–25—Save 10 percent for the future.

- Romans 13:8—Pay your bills. (Several pretend bills were listed, such as $500 for the house payment, $150 for food, and $150 for the car.)

Once the large cash pile was counted and broken into smaller "Give," "Save," and "Bills" piles, we counted the remaining money. Each child was given one dollar to spend. Needless to say, they were a bit disappointed. But they also better understood the real-world expenses of life, as well as our responsibilities as stewards of the money God gives. We ended our time together by creating a Stewardship Box with three slots labeled "Give," "Save," and "Spend" for the kids to use when they earn money and also memorizing our little jingle for the evening: *Before you spend away—give, save, and pay.*

CASH IN HAND

To help your children learn delayed gratification with regard to money, establish a rule that the kids can spend money on items they want only when they have the cash to do so. This will develop a pattern of learning the discipline and rewards of saving money until there is enough for an important purchase rather than wasting it on little things and "borrowing" from Mom and Dad to buy the big stuff. This is a very important and difficult habit to learn in a culture that has gone wild with credit spending—all the more reason to instill the discipline when our children are young.

A GIVING BIRTHDAY PARTY

Just before your children's next birthdays, talk to them about throwing a party that is about giving rather than getting. Your children can ask everyone who attends to bring money for a special charity or a gift for ministries that send Christmas presents to third-world children. You can always buy your children a nice present yourself so they have something to open themselves. But they can also experience the lasting joy of knowing they celebrated the blessing of their own birth by blessing someone less fortunate.

CHAPTER SIX

Fostering
Total Dependence

(Deadly Sin: Sloth)

Every parent experiences an occasional twinge of sorrow at the realization that kids grow up fast. It usually occurs while carrying a sleeping child from the car to his or her upstairs bedroom. Your little boy used to be so easy to pick up, but suddenly he feels as heavy as a sack of potatoes. Your daughter once nestled her chubby cheeks against your face while ascending the steps, tiny feet dangling over your rib cage. Now her body drapes down your entire midsection and her size-five shoes hang too far below your belly to remove en route. Yesterday morning your child slept peacefully in an infant car seat. This afternoon he'll ask you to drive him to soccer practice. Tomorrow, she'll want help picking out her wedding dress. Where does the time go?

It's called *the empty nest*, that dreaded season when the job of providing for and nurturing kids comes to an end and we achieve *parent emeritus* status. Those of us still living in the minivan years can hardly imagine the possibility, but a day is coming when the children will no longer need us to tuck them in bed, pack their lunches, lay out their clothes, or clean up their dishes. And, as nice as that may sound today, we will feel sad over the close of a life stage that defined our existence—and affirmed our worth.

But it doesn't have to be that way. We could learn from parents like Al and Sue. Their thirty-something son, Tripp, never put his mom and dad through the pain of separation. Sue still lays out his clothes, cleans his dishes, and packs him a lunch. And while Tripp doesn't need to be tucked in at night, he does still appreciate Mom's preparing him a nice home-cooked meal and bedtime snack.

Unlike other parents who feel the twinge of regret when kids leave home, Al and Sue find themselves wondering when—if ever—their boy will strike out on his own. Instead of an empty nest, they face a cluttered nest, crowded by a full-grown bird refusing to stretch his wings and fly.

If he lived in Japan, Tripp would be labeled a "parasite single"—someone in his late twenties or early thirties who lives with his parents and enjoys a carefree and comfortable life. The term was popularized by a university professor in Tokyo who studied the growing cultural phenomenon.[1] Many of these young "adults" don't even help with household chores or pay rent. Some even continue to receive an allowance for spending money. The growth in the number of "parasite singles" corresponds to an increase in the average age of the first marriage, which has risen from about twenty-one in 1960 to today's twenty-seven years old.[2]

A reluctance to marry certainly plays a part in Tripp's reluctance to leave home. A good-looking guy, he likes having a girlfriend willing to share his bed. But he has no interest in anyone's sharing his life. The commitment of marriage is way too grown-up for Tripp's liking. So he has as much fun as possible until relationships turn serious. The moment a girl appears to be falling in love, Tripp invites her to "his place" so that she can discover that he still lives with his parents, lose all respect for him, and storm out of the relationship. Success! Another potential commitment averted, allowing Tripp to move on to the next girl.

Al and Sue play an important part in Tripp's pattern. Psychologists would call them *enablers*. But Tripp calls them terrific parents!

Al and Sue are characters in the 2006 film *Failure to Launch* starring Matthew McConaughey, who plays

Tripp, a grown man who won't grow up, work hard, or support himself. And while the story may be fiction, the reality it portrays has become more common, thanks to moms and dads who have mastered the process of fostering a spirit of total dependence in their children.

The Ties That Bind and Blind

Of course, not every adult who lives with his or her parents can be called a parasite. But the word does conjure up a helpful image for mess-up parenting. Dig out your high school biology textbook and you'll find that a parasite is a living organism that survives by draining life and resources from another, usually larger organism. Not a pretty picture, but one that best characterizes the downhill tendency of a deadly sin known as *sloth*—the one character quality essential to helping our kids join the ranks of those who take more than they give and expect others to carry their load.

Dr. Ruby Payne is widely acknowledged as a leading expert on the subject of how parents' financial patterns influence their children. Whether one finds himself in poverty, the middle class, or wealth depends in large part on how his parents viewed money, time, and destiny.[3] The wealthy, for example, see money as something to be conserved and invested. The middle class see it as something to be managed, while the poor view money as something to be spent.

Dr. M. Scott Peck explains the pattern in his best-selling book *The Road Less Traveled*:

> They are the "Do as I say, not as I do" parents. . . . They may be slovenly. They make promises they don't keep. Their own lives are frequently and obviously in disorder and disarray, and their attempts to order the lives of their children seem therefore to make little sense to these children. . . . If a child sees his parents day in and day out living without self-restraint or self-discipline, then he will come in the deepest fibers of being to believe that that is the way to live.[4]

Of course, parasites come in all shapes, sizes, and economic situations. A spoiled child of wealth living in the lap of luxury feels just as entitled as the welfare recipient who refuses to work. Both, after all, are looking for the next handout. Nothing binds us to irresponsibility or blinds us to possibilities like an entitlement mind-set. And no one is better equipped to instill that attitude into the next generation than dear old Mom and Dad.

Conventional Wisdom

Uphill advocates consider sloth among the most serious deadly sins because it cuts the legs out from under the potential climber. To understand why, we need to understand what conventional wisdom has to say on the subject.

The traditional definition of *sloth* is "a hatred of all spiritual things which entail effort" and "faintheartedness in matters of difficulty."[5] We typically think of sloth as laziness, and it is. But this deadly sin murders more than our initiative to work. It reaches its wilting hand much farther, ultimately killing our will to live. Let's consider a few of its effects in our lives.

LAZINESS

The book of Proverbs is filled with admonitions to work hard, pursue wisdom, and invest one's life in things that matter, laying aside immediate gratification for the long-term rewards of diligence. It is no wonder, then, that it speaks ill of idleness.

Solomon characterizes the lazy as someone who manages to come up with plenty of excuses for remaining idle: "A sluggard is wiser in his own eyes than seven men who answer discreetly" (Prov. 26:16).

Ask him to get up and get busy, for example, and the lazy man says, "There is a lion in the road, a fierce lion roaming the streets!" (Prov. 26:13). Never mind that everyone else is out and about. Never mind that the reported lion turns out to be a false rumor. The remote possibility is good enough for the lazy to hit the snooze button over and over again. "As a door turns on its hinges," continues Solomon, "so a sluggard turns on his bed" (Prov. 26:14).

A midrash (a rabbinical commentary) on this portion of Scripture offers a more detailed play-by-play description of the sluggard's hesitancy: When told he must travel to town to get his lesson from his Torah teacher, the sluggard replies, "But I fear the lion in the way." When told he is very close to the house, the sluggard persists, "I fear that the lion may be in the streets." When informed the teacher is in his house, the sluggard says, "I am certain to find the door bolted." When told the door is open, the sluggard runs out of "legitimate" excuses and is forced to 'fess up. "Whether the door is open or bolted, I want to sleep just a little longer."[6]

His reply brings to mind another of Solomon's proverbs:

> How long will you lie there, you sluggard?
>   When will you get up from your sleep?
> A little sleep, a little slumber,
>   a little folding of the hands to rest—
> and poverty will come on you like a bandit.
>
>   (Proverbs 6:9–11)

The apostle Paul also took a dim view of idleness as expressed in letters written to leaders of the early church. To a young pastor named Timothy he wrote, "If anyone does not provide for his relatives, and especially for his immediate family, he has denied the faith and is worse than an unbeliever" (1 Tim. 5:8). He even went so far as to exclude younger widows from taking advantage of the benevolence budget unless they were willing to work (1 Tim. 5:11–13).

In another situation Paul discovered that several parasites refused to carry their weight among the Christians in Thessalonica. So he restated a basic rule: "'If a man will not work, he shall not eat.' We hear that some among you are idle. . . . Such people we command and urge in the Lord Jesus Christ to settle down and earn the bread they eat" (2 Thess. 3:10–12).

The Scriptures clearly condemn laziness. That's one of the reasons our grandparents gave children chores. It might have been less hassle to do the work themselves. But they saw hard work as a weapon against the kind of downhill drift that leads to a sluggard's snooze button.

PROCRASTINATION

Another manifestation of the deadly sin of sloth is our tendency to procrastinate. *Procrastination* is just a fancy word for avoiding what we ought to do. Of course, we fully intend to do the right thing. We will get to it, one of these days. But for some strange reason that day never seems to come.

You might call procrastination *bite-size laziness.* To totally neglect our responsibilities might cause shame. But to put them off a bit, waiting for inspiration to propel us into action, now that's a sin we can feel good about! Or at least feel less bad about.

Nobody sets out to become a failure. We arrive there one "I'll get to it" at a time. Procrastination pushes the hard stuff aside so we can enjoy the moment, which is precisely the opposite of what M. Scott Peck says brings success—delaying gratification. "Delaying gratification is a process of scheduling the pain and pleasure of life in such a way as to enhance the pleasure by meeting and experiencing the pain first and getting it over with. It is the only decent way to live."[7]

When we do the difficult thing first, we reap the fruit of that discipline later. At least that's how it is supposed to work. When we delay gratification, we move little by little toward success. Procrastination, on the other hand, moves us little by little in the other direction.

A support Web site for procrastinators poses several questions to those who stop by looking for help: "Are you a chronic procrastinator? Do you struggle with Internet or video game addiction? In times of stress do you find yourself daydreaming, watching TV, or engaging in anything to avoid what you are supposed to be doing? Do you have a '*T*otally *D*readed' list instead of a '*T*o-*D*o' list?"[8]

To those who might answer yes to such questions, Solomon points to the example of a bug:

> Go to the ant, you sluggard;
>> consider his ways and be wise!
> It has no commander,
>> no overseer or ruler,
> yet it stores its provisions in summer
>> and gathers its food at harvest.
>
> (Proverbs 6:6–8)

The ant takes initiative to do the wise thing, not because he is forced or threatened. He does it because, unlike us humans, he doesn't have a deadly disease called *sloth*.

DESPONDENCY

Seventeenth-century Christian apologist Blaise Pascal described a third deadly manifestation of sloth when he wrote, "Nothing is so insufferable to man as to be completely at rest, without passions, without business, without diversion, without study." In such a condition, man "feels his nothingness, his forlornness, his insufficiency, his dependence, his weakness, his emptiness. There will immediately arise from the depth of his heart weariness, gloom, sadness, fretfulness, vexation, despair."[9]

Many fail to connect the dots between idleness and its life-killing lover, despondency. Physical laziness is, according to Solomon Schimmel,

> a small part of what sloth referred to in the past. The sin of sloth has two components: *acadia*, which means lack of caring, an aimless indifference to one's responsibilities to God and to man, and *tristitia*, meaning sadness and sorrow. . . . Sloth, then, is the loss of one's spiritual moorings in life and the ensuing spiritual vacuum manifests itself in despondency, and flight from the worship of God and service to man.[10]

Schimmel rightfully points out that sadness and apathy can be both the cause and the result of avoiding responsibility.

It seems more than coincidental that the dramatic rise in depression and low self-esteem of the past generation corresponds to the dramatic rise in the amount of time we spend on leisure. Oh, sure, we are busier than ever, but activity does not equal diligence. Our schedules are packed because one of sloth's favorite tricks is to hide under the cover of business. As Ken Bazyn put it, "It's not that the slothful are inactive, but the tasks they do perform seem so second-rate."[11] We could also add *so unimportant*.

The very word for *bored* did not exist in premodern

languages.[12] "Of course not," we might respond. "They were so busy just trying to put food on the table they didn't have room in their days to think about how miserable they were." Precisely the point. Moderns can't imagine a life so filled with labor. In what would seem a reversal to past generations, we find identity in our distractions and resent our duties. Many of us consider ourselves overworked if we can't make it home from work in time for that hit game show or from church in time to see the kickoff. We spend very little time pursuing noble purposes and a whole lot of it pointing the television remote or computer mouse to "surf" our way into boredom.

Boredom, which is another manifestation of sloth, is a sworn enemy of the kind of life Christ called us into. "The thief comes only to steal and kill and destroy; I have come that they may have life, and have it to the full" (John 10:10).

The further we move down sloth's slippery slope, the further we get from the purpose for which we were made: to know and glorify God. The momentum of apathy overtakes our spirits until what started as a way of dismissing our responsibility to God and others overtakes our very will to live. Solomon describes what happens to such a person consumed by despondency: "The sluggard buries his hand in the dish; he is too lazy to bring it back to his mouth" (Prov. 26:15).

Why bother eating when I'm so bored with life I see

no need to go on? The same apathetic yawn that keeps a sluggard's hand from bringing food to his or her mouth also steals the motivation to work hard at a job, find a husband or wife, learn a skill, invest for the future, read a book, raise a child, or even go to the dentist. The despondency of sloth considers such options and lethargically mumbles, "I'd rather not."

Conventional wisdom calls the slothful to leave their passive boredom and embrace a life of passionate diligence. One nineteenth-century prayer book invited the apathetic into worship in order to "stir up the dull mind of man to the remembrance of his duty to God."[13] And, in what may be the best anecdote for sloth ever concocted, John Wesley is commonly credited with having given early Methodists this rule of conduct:

> Do all the good you can,
> By all the means you can,
> In all the ways you can,
> In all the places you can,
> At all the times you can,
> To all the people you can,
> As long as you can.[14]

Prior generations considered diligence vital to one's well-being. When we fulfill our obligations, they thought, we discover our purpose. They saw personal responsibility and the diligence it requires as a tether preventing a free fall into an abyss of an endless pursuit of personal gratification.

Mess-Up Strategies

"Parenthood shrivels," writes Mark Rutland, "because it takes discipline to lovingly train another. It is easier to indulge a child than to shape his character. . . . Chastening, teaching, rebuking, and even properly punishing a child takes time, perseverance and sacrifice. To give him what he pleads and weeps and screams for costs very little."[15] Exactly! And that's why mess-up moms and dads take the path of least resistance rather than wear themselves out moving children toward self-reliance and personal responsibility. How? By following some of these simple strategies.

MESS-UP STRATEGY #1: GET OFF THEIR BACKS

Children can be very creative and persistent when it comes to avoiding work. If you've ever tried to get them to pause the video game, turn off the television, or hang up the cell phone in order to make their beds, help with the dishes, mow the lawn, or do their homework—you know what a hassle it can be.

"But I need to finish this level before turning off the game!" protests your son.

"I emptied the dishwasher last month. Why do I always have to do it?" reasons your little princess.

The defenses are endless. . . .

- Why do I need to make my bed anyway? I'm just going to mess it up again tonight.

- Susan's parents let her talk to her friends on the phone as much as she wants. I wish I lived in her family!

- Do I have to do it right this minute? I've never seen this episode and need to find out how SpongeBob resolves his relationship with Patrick.

- It's a stupid assignment anyway.

- I was going to do it, but I forgot. What's the big deal?

- Can you just get off my back?

Mess-up parents take that suggestion to heart. They back off and let their kids relax. They enable children to avoid or delay anything that requires hard work, personal discipline, or deferred gratification. After all, such activities put children at risk of success—undermining their progress toward parasite-hood.

MESS-UP STRATEGY #2: DO IT YOURSELF

You walk past your children's bedrooms and notice the floors littered with toys, clothes, or used tissues. Your first instinct is to find the children and insist they clean up the mess. The problem with this approach, of course, is the time and effort required, especially if your children are prone to overreaction. Mess-up parents have learned a valuable lesson when confronted with the messy-room scenario: it is much easier to simply do it themselves. In five minutes they can tidy up the room and move on with their day, especially if they are angry, since fury can accelerate the process.

To make the children clean up, by contrast, could stretch the effort to an hour-long ordeal. You must calm yourself down, then locate Junior and Missy and disengage them from whatever they might be doing. You will ask how many times you've told them to clean up their mess and then tell them to clean up their mess. Upon reaching the room and seeing for themselves that the room does indeed look like a bomb went off, they will likely flop themselves on the floor in tortured agony over the unreasonable scope of the job. After several rounds of argument and threats, you will give in and help pick up since, in the children's words, "It will take me forever to do this all by myself!"

Just do it yourself. Not only will you find it less stressful, your children will learn to let others do the hard stuff while they stick to fun and games. After all, messed-up children learn early that it is better to put off until tomorrow what your mom might do for you today.

MESS-UP STRATEGY #3: PITY THE CHILD

Experts disagree on whether despondency causes laziness or the other way around. It probably works both ways, giving mess-up parents yet another strategy to help kids roll down the slope of sloth. When your children feel down in the dumps, make sure to help them stay there. Remember, apathy often disguises itself as depression.

The opportunities generally reveal themselves when Mom or Dad suggests some real-life activity that requires action. It could be work, like a chore—or play, like a fun family outing. Watch for a passive yawn, rolling eyes, or an inattentive stare. Such body language might also be accompanied by a statement like "I don't really feel up to it right now" or "Can I bow out? I'm not in the mood to be with anyone."

You might be tempted to push the children past such moments, considering them mere pity parties that need a splash of cold water rather than a cuddly, warm blanket. Don't go there. When children begin feeling sorry for themselves—lying around doing nothing meaningful, demonstrating that "I could care less" attitude—they are well on their way to the final stages of sloth. The last thing they need from Mom or Dad is a kick in the pants or a pep talk. All they need is a little bit of compassion and a little bit of space. Mess-up parents leave the children be so their despondency can properly fester.

MESS-UP STRATEGY #4: ACCEPT MEDIOCRITY

Nothing requires more hard work from parents than demanding excellence from a child. We must follow-through and follow-up. Our advice: don't. The world is filled with mediocre adults accomplishing less than they could. Why not give your kids a jump on the competition by expecting mediocrity during childhood?

Taking Precautions

For those determined to mess up their children's lives by fostering the deadly sin of sloth, increase your odds by ignoring the following suggestions designed to instill the virtue of diligence.

> ### WARNING:
> *The following ideas could be hazardous to*
> *the process of messing up your child's life.*
> *Read at your own risk!*

STEWARDSHIP BLOCKS

To teach your kids the importance of being good stewards of their time, cut a piece of wood into eight to ten blocks of various sizes. Make sure the total length when laid end to end is greater than the length of a household coffee or dining table. On each block, write one of the following words representing the various activities that could fill time in the child's day: chores, sleeping, eating, school, playing, computer game time, watching television, reading, bathing, and so on. Write the less-important items (television, computer games) on the shorter blocks, and the essential items (eating, sleeping) on the longer blocks.

Invite each child to the "24 Hour" table and ask them to place the blocks on the table in the order of what they like to do. They will quickly discover that there is not enough room on the table for several of the really important blocks. Discuss the items left over, and ask what the impact on life would be if there were not enough time to eat, bathe, and go to school. Next, ask them to place the blocks on the "24 Hour" table in order of importance. They will find that several of the "like to do" blocks will not fit on the table. Share that this is like life: we have a limited amount of time, and we must carefully select and prioritize how we will spend that time—making certain to do the important things before the fun things. There will be time for all the fun things, but maybe not every day. Read Ecclesiastes 3:1 and the parable in Matthew 25:14–29 and discuss ways to implement this principle in your home.

ENDURANCE

If you are really nuts, try this activity. Place a large bucket of very cold water and floating ice in front of your children with several dozen marbles in the bottom. Tell the kids that you will pay a quarter for every marble the kids can pull out of the water with their toes in three minutes or less. They will jump at the opportunity to torture themselves for a few minutes in order to reap the rewards of several dollars.

Once the retrieval is completed, ask the kids (who will likely be holding blue feet) to explain why they did such a painful thing. "For the money" will come the reply. "So you looked beyond the short-term pain in order to gain the long-term reward?"

Point made. When we look beyond the short-term pain or inconvenience of doing what is hard, we can reap the rewards that come from self-discipline and delayed gratification!

LONG-TERM PROJECT

A simple way to reinforce the value of delayed gratification is to plan a long-term project as a family that will require several weeks or months to complete a little at a time: building a toy box, painting the basement, landscaping the yard, or organizing the garage. Identify a reward for the entire family once the task is completed: a camping trip, a professional ball game, or some activity that will motivate everyone. Once completed, enjoy the anticipated reward together in celebration of the commitment and discipline required to succeed.

MOVIE NIGHT: *RUDY*

Based on the true story of Dan "Rudy" Ruettiger, this film is a powerful picture of determination to accomplish the unlikely through personal discipline and hard work. A poor student and mediocre athlete, Rudy has a dream of someday playing football for the University of Notre Dame. Four years after high school graduation, Rudy finds himself working in the steel mill with his father and brother, his dream unrealized. After an accident that takes the life of his best friend, Rudy heads to South Bend to pursue his dream—only to discover his grades are inadequate to get into Notre Dame. As this inspiring story unfolds, Rudy disciplines himself to overcome incredible obstacles in order to reach his goal. Here are a few questions to draw out some key lessons of this film:

> *Question:* What were some of the obstacles Rudy had to overcome in order to achieve his dream?

Answer: Poor grades, being small, being poor, a family that didn't believe in him, etc.

Question: What were the most important qualities Rudy displayed in order to overcome each of these obstacles?

Answer: Determination, self-discipline, and hard work.

Question: What was so special about his accomplishment?

Answer: He gained a sense of self-respect and he broke out of the cycle of complacency his family was trapped in.

Question: What Bible passage does this film illustrate well?

Answer: Proverbs 13:4.

JOBS BASKET

Create a family jobs basket with small sheets of paper each describing one task that needs to be done. Set aside one day per month for completing everything in the basket. Each family member must take turns selecting a job until they are all gone. Plan to treat the entire family to something special that evening once everything is done (a movie, ice cream, a red convertible sports car). Some of the jobs will be bigger than others, and certain children may consider their stack unfair. But the rule of the day is "You pick it, you do it." Allow no complaining. This system keeps you caught up on periodic household duties, and it teaches kids that every member of the family must be responsible to pitch in and help. (This is most effective for kids ages seven to sixteen.)

CHAPTER SEVEN

Condoning Sensual Gratification

(Deadly Sin: Lust)

The film intended to make a statement, featuring the very different lives of two siblings—brother and sister. He is a nerdy fellow who spends every spare moment watching reruns of his favorite television show. Attracted to the ideal world it presents, the boy dreams of one day living a life as perfect as those in the black-and-white paradise called Pleasantville. She, on the other hand, likes life as it is. Attractive, cool, and popular with the boys—partly because she is willing to sleep around—the last place on earth the sister would want to live is that goody-two-shoes world her geeky brother idolizes. No sir, she prefers life loose and fast.

As the story unfolds, both brother and sister end up in Pleasantville. They, like everyone else, are forced to live in a black-and-white world. It is a world that knows nothing of color or the passion it symbolizes. That is, until the sister decides to educate them on how to "really" have fun!

Before long, teens begin having sex, women leave domineering husbands, and the mother exchanges a mundane marriage for the excitement of an extramarital affair. In short, people begin to experience what life beyond Pleasantville can be. In the process, their black-and-white world gradually turns to brilliant color. Free from the constraints of goody-two-shoes living, the residents of Pleasantville begin to embrace the wonders and excitement of a passion they've never known.

The only problem is a few stick-in-the-mud folks who want to get rid of the "coloreds" and return Pleasantville to the way it was. They liked the world bland and predictable—as it should be! In the end, however, passion wins out, and the entire community accepts color as something good.

The statement of the film *Pleasantville* is obvious: When we free people from the constraints of an outdated value system, they can discover the colorful world of passion. The problem with our culture is not those who promote sensual indulgence and sexual freedom. The problem is those who would keep us from finding and fulfilling our desires.

Of course, the film's message is the complete opposite of reality. Sin, not purity, robs life of passion and color by turning it into a bland and colorless existence. The short-term thrill of illicit sex is quickly replaced by the guilt and consequences that come when we leave the protective parameters of innocence. But our generation cannot comprehend the wonders of passion experienced in the context of purity. It sees any limits on expression as something that steals enjoyment rather than increases its intensity.

A Porn Generation

Twenty-year-old Harvard Law School student Ben Shapiro wrote an alarmingly instructive book for parents titled *Porn Generation: How Social Liberalism Is Corrupting Our Future*. He details the kind of world the sexual revolution, a baby-boomer legacy, has created for their grandkids. Needless to say, it is no Pleasantville.

"When the stigma left sexual licentiousness," explains Shapiro, "society felt the sting in rising rates of teen pregnancy, sexually transmitted disease, emotional emptiness, and nihilism." While the hallmark of baby boomers was rebellion, he continues, "the hallmark of my generation is jadedness."[1] That's largely because when it comes to pursuing sexual gratification, our children are being fed a lie they all too willingly believe.

The slope of humanity descends steeply downhill when it comes to our sensuality—giving parents yet another opportunity for messing up their children's lives.

Conventional Wisdom

Viewing lust as a deadly sin goes way back in history. We all know adultery made it onto the top ten list Moses carried down from the mountain. But lust as vice extends to nonreligious thought as well. The philosopher Aristotle, for example, contrasted the vice of licentiousness (another word for *lust*) with the virtue of temperance. He criticized the lustful man as one who becomes so carried away by desire that he chooses sexual pleasure over anything else in life. He even compared the licentious person to a spoiled child because both need to submit their appetites for pleasure to authority.[2]

That's why so many frown upon the sexual revolution as undermining a traditional perspective on human sexuality. It tore down the protective guidelines of sexual expression, confusing love with passion and gratification with fulfillment. During the same era, radical feminism fanned confusion over what it means to be made in God's image as distinctly male or female. The result is a generation trapped in a bland, colorless world, seeking to satisfy a yearning that can be filled only through the wonders of biblical sexuality.

Christopher West, author of *Naked Without Shame*, says the way to find out what is most sacred in this world is to "look for what is most violently profaned."[3] Junior high boys and stand-up comics don't invent lewd words about a person's elbow or earlobe. They use foul language only when describing those parts of our bodies that distinguish the sexes. We don't hear many dirty stories about a person's respiratory system or digestive system in action. But go into any locker room and you'll hear plenty of distasteful language about parts of the reproductive system. Why? Because sex is sacred—making it our enemy's primary target for defamation.

Biblical Sex

So what is a Christian view of human sexuality? Several Scripture passages paint the picture:

- "God created man in his own image, in the image of God he created him; male and female he created them" (Gen. 1:27). In short, each of us was made male or female as a specific reflection of God's own image. And, in some mysterious way, when we join together "as one flesh" in holy matrimony, the two merge into an icon of God's relationship with humanity.

- "'For this reason a man will leave his father and mother and be united to his wife, and the two shall become one flesh.' This is a profound mystery—but I am talking about Christ and the church. However, each one of you also must love his wife as he loves himself, and the wife must respect her husband" (Eph. 5:31–33). Sadly, the beauty of that image becomes an ugly distortion when we make sex an idol to our own self-satisfaction rather than an icon of God's selfless love.

- "God gave them over in the sinful desires of their hearts to sexual impurity for the degrading of their bodies with one another. They exchanged the truth of God for a lie, and worshiped and served created things rather than the Creator. . . . Because of this, God gave them over to shameful lusts" (Rom. 1:24–26). The good news, of course, is that marriage provides a context for sexual fulfillment that is at once healthy and exciting, wholesome, and really, really fun!

With the exception of those called to a lifelong celibacy, most of our children should pursue God-honoring marriages that will both express the beauty of God's love and protect them from sliding down the hill of sexual degradation.

- "Since there is so much immorality, each man should have his own wife, and each woman her own husband. The husband should fulfill his marital duty to his wife, and likewise the wife to her husband. The wife's body does not belong to her alone but also to her husband. In the same way, the husband's body does not belong to him alone but also to his wife. Do not deprive each other except by mutual consent and for a time, so that you may devote yourselves to prayer. Then come together again so that Satan will not tempt you because of your lack of self-control" (1 Cor. 7:2–5).

Even those who don't commit what traditional religion calls *fornication* can find themselves ensnared in the deadly sin of lust. In fact, Jesus raised the bar on conventional wisdom when He told holier-than-thou religious leaders, "Anyone who looks at a woman lustfully has already committed adultery with her in his heart" (Matt. 5:28). Apparently the only qualification necessary for condemnation on this one is having a pulse. Boys look lustfully, and girls enjoy being looked at. So, according to conventional wisdom, "Houston, we have a problem!"

Lack of Self-Control

What does conventional wisdom say about what happens when we lack self-control? It is not a pretty picture.

A tearful young woman takes a long shower, trying to wash away the shame she feels after her first illicit encounter. Be it the abuse of rape or voluntary infidelity, the loss of sexual innocence makes her feel dirty, violated, ashamed. But that same girl will have a very different reaction after a year of prostitution. A cold stare tells you her heart is resigned to the shame that now defines her existence. A seductive glance suggests an acquired taste for erotic pleasures. Dark shadows under her eyes and deep facial lines invade the soft, graceful beauty she once possessed. And loud, brazen laughter overtakes the gentle, pretty smile that was so charming just twelve months earlier.

When first introduced to the illicit pleasures of sin, there was a sick feeling in the pit of her stomach. Her innocence had been violated: she'd been raped by a villain or seduced by an adulterous lover. She was, at first, ashamed. But before long, she forgot what innocence was like and began preferring her fallen state.

The downhill pattern of sin causes us to crave that which should make us cry. The human race has been living in bondage to lust for so long that we cannot even remember the thrilling excitement and passion found in purity. Celebrating our addictions, we view them as keys of liberation rather than chains of enslavement.

In C. S. Lewis's fictitious series of letters between two demons, the elder Screwtape advises his nephew

Wormwood on how to use God's invention of pleasure against us:

> Never forget that when we are dealing with any pleasure in its healthy and normal and satisfying form, we are, in a sense, on the Enemy's ground. I know we have won many a soul through pleasure. All the same, it is His intention, not ours. . . . Hence we always try to work away from the natural condition of any pleasure to that in which it is least natural, least redolent of its Maker, and least pleasurable. An ever increasing craving for an ever diminishing pleasure is the formula.[4]

This is the reality of every person born on earth. We all experience the enticement and enslavement of sin pulling us deeper into the abyss of self-gratification. "An ever increasing craving for an ever diminishing pleasure": an ugly image indeed.

We have made sex about individual gratification, expressed in our pornography and culture of casual sex. When sex becomes about me, others exist to satisfy my whims, be they *Playboy* nudes, streetwalking prostitutes, or abused children. The thought of God is the last thing we want invading our sexual thoughts.

Others have made sex a necessary evil, a guilt-inducing embarrassment, or a wicked indulgence. God could have made human sexuality more like that of animals, giving males the urge only around females in heat. Children could be conceived while keeping desire and pleasure to a minimum. Or sex could have been a sweet and loving experience without the hassle of erotic urges. This certainly would have eliminated the abuses of premarital fornication, extramarital adultery, and e-mail porn ads. But for some reason, God made sex intensely pleasurable. He made it something we can't help desiring or stop pursuing (again, unless He's called us to lifelong celibacy). He made it something we can choose to enjoy either within the healthy parameters of fidelity or as a disease-ridden obsession.

At its best, sex is about intimacy between two individuals, each trying to please the other. Personal gratification is a gift received, not an entitlement taken.

At its best, sex is a very private experience within the security of an exclusive relationship. Despite our ravings to the contrary, we all long for that ideal: one man with one woman, enjoying faithful intimacy in all its forms, for a lifetime.

At its best, sex gives and receives guilt-free pleasure within the parameters of marital fidelity. Expressions outside that protective fence become physically, emotionally, and spiritually reckless, with potentially deadly consequences.

Mess-Up Strategies

Not that we need much coaching on this one, but there are a few tips mess-up parents might find helpful as they seek to accelerate their children's tendency toward sensual gratification.

MESS-UP STRATEGY #1: EXPECT FAILURE

You might have "gone too far" with the opposite sex when you were young and foolish: perhaps a make-out party during junior high, heavy petting while watching a movie, or much more. You were only doing what came naturally, so to speak. And mess-up parents expect no better from their kids. In fact, they expect far worse.

Unlike our grandparents, most in our generation view adolescent kids as animals in heat unable to control their "primal urges." And who can blame us? We have been told the best approach to preventing unwanted pregnancy and venereal disease is to distribute condoms. The quaint old advice "Say no!" has been replaced by the more progressive "Be safe!" Doing so, of course, becomes a self-fulfilling prophecy by reinforcing the message: *Try as you might, you won't be able to resist temptation.*

In the old days parents (and their churches) taught kids to heed biblical warnings about fornication and considered failure the exception rather than the rule.

That's because they expected their children to live like people made in the image of God, possessing enough common sense and willpower to "flee . . . youthful lusts" (2 Tim. 2:22 KJV). But about 27 percent of today's kids self-report engaging in premarital sexual intimacy.[5] Many experts believe that percentage has skyrocketed in recent years precisely because adults expect no better and treat young people accordingly. Mess-up parents go with the flow on this one, helping their own children adopt a defeatist attitude when it comes to sexual temptation.

MESS-UP STRATEGY #2: OVERREACT

Let's face it: sex is an awkward subject to discuss with our kids. That's one of the reasons mess-up parents do so in the worst possible moments in the worst possible ways. Rather than having a planned, purposeful discussion on the birds, the bees, and babies, many find themselves conducting their first conversation in reaction to a surprise invasion of the topic.

In our case, the topic first emerged when our oldest came home from his fourth-grade class and asked why we hate happy people.

"What are you talking about?" asked Kurt, looking perplexed. "We don't hate happy people."

"Well," responded our son, "a girl in my class said that you hate gay people. I didn't know what that meant so I looked up the word in the dictionary. It means 'happy.' " (As you probably figured out, the little girl lived with "two mommies" [lesbian lovers], and they accused Christians of hating them because we believe marriage is between a man and a woman.)

Suddenly, before we had even considered explaining sex to our fourth-grade son—we got hit with the need to explain homosexuality.

While you may not be accused of hating happy people, something will likely catch you off guard, triggering a conversation about sex. It might be a television commercial that piques a child's curiosity. Or it could be a bad word, a dirty joke, or a child's misspeaking that suddenly throws you into reaction mode.

In such moments, mess-up parents react in perplexed horror that such a naughty topic has reared its ugly head. Through body language, expressions of shocked embarrassment, and disapproving looks, they communicate a very simple message: *Sex is an evil taboo that should not be discussed in polite company—or anyplace else, for heaven's sake!*

As the child gets a bit older, other opportunities to overreact will surface, such as the first time you discover they have seen online pornography: "What are you, some sort of pervert? I can't believe a young man who calls himself a Christian would look at such images!"

Or when your adolescent daughter tries on a "cute" outfit that reveals she has become a shapely young lady who will turn boys' heads: "For heaven's sake! I will not have any daughter of mine walking around in public in an outfit that makes her look like a lady of the night!"

The key is overreacting to such situations in a way that causes the child to think of all sexuality as bad, dirty, and worthy of shame rather than thinking sex is good with balanced biblical boundaries and guidance.

MESS-UP STRATEGY #3: UNDERREACT

For those who can't quite bring themselves to treat sex as totally taboo, it is equally effective to use the other extreme. Rather than overreact to all sexuality, under-react to all dangers. This is, perhaps, the easiest way to accelerate a child's downhill tendency. A few examples might be helpful.

• When setting up your Internet service at home, avoid using any sort of Web-filtering software or password-protected access. Better yet, let your son have his own computer behind the closed door of his bedroom. Rest in the hope he will have no interest in the pornographic images readily available online. And even if he does, treat it as harmless curiosity rather than a po-tential addiction.

• When your daughter reaches the age when she becomes attracted to boys, be sure to let her buy and wear the latest fashions regardless of how revealing or alluring they might be. After all, every girl wants to be wanted—and the "right look" can turn heads!

• When your son's crush on the school cheerleader turns into an invitation to join her at an after-game party, don't put any pressure on him to resist temptation if she makes an advance. After all, "fleeing youthful lusts" can be embarrassing—especially when she is willing and everyone else is doing it.

• When your fourteen-year-old daughter gets asked out on her first date by a much older boy, let her go have a good time. The stars in her eyes don't necessarily mean she is too immature to resist potential sexual advances. She might only let him go as far as second or third base.

In short, ignore the suggestion that sex is like gas and temptation a match. They might just maintain their purity without your saying or doing a thing.

Taking Precautions

For those determined to mess up their children's lives by fostering the deadly sin of lust, increase your odds by ignoring the following suggestions designed to instill the virtue of chastity.

> **WARNING:**
> *The following ideas could be hazardous to the process of messing up your child's life. Read at your own risk!*

AFFIRMING DIFFERENCES

One of the most important things we can do to give our children a healthy sense of sexual identity is to affirm the differences between sexes. In order to do so, capitalize on critical events in the lives of your kids: dinner and shopping with Mom to celebrate daughter's first bra; a weekend trip to celebrate her "becoming a woman day" (otherwise known as her first menstruation). For boys, other events serve as great opportunities to reinforce sexual identity, such as that first hit in a baseball game or first job (whether mowing lawns or a paper route). Take your daughter shopping to buy a frilly new dress when younger, or a cute outfit when older, so that she can feel feminine and pretty. Bring your son to a professional game and let him admire the strength and aggression that are uniquely masculine and part of the image of God in man. Verbally praise the uniquely masculine or feminine qualities in Dad and Mom in front of the children. Here are some examples:

> DAD ABOUT MOM: "I think Mom is the prettiest girl in the world. I'm lucky she is my date!" or "Mom has such soft skin—I love to touch it!"
>
> MOM ABOUT DAD: "You'll have to ask Daddy to lift that—he is stronger than Mommy."

PURITY CELEBRATION

Thirteen-year-old Rachael plans to remain sexually pure until her wedding night. She made a formal commitment to that goal at the start of puberty one year ago. Her parents arranged a special ceremony for her, which they called A Celebration of Purity. The family dressed up, gathered for a formal banquet—the menu and program were printed and placed on each plate. The order of celebration included dinner (featuring Mama), ceremony (featuring Papa, Mama, Grandpa and Grandma, and close family friends), special music, signing of the Purity Covenant Certificate, and presentation of a covenant gift.

With the exception of her actual wedding ceremony, nothing will make a greater impression on Rachael of the beauty and purity of God's design for sexuality.

LETTER TO FUTURE SPOUSE

When your children reach the appropriate level of maturity, help them write letters to the people they hope to marry someday. Encourage them to tell about their family, their interests, their hopes and dreams, and about the commitment they are making to remain pure so that they can experience the wonder and excitement of sexual intimacy with him or her alone. This letter can become a powerful symbol and tangible reminder of the importance of remaining pure during the temptation-filled teen years.

PREPARING FOR ADOLESCENCE WEEKEND

Over the past few decades, thousands of parents have confronted the birds-and-the-bees discussion in a creative and effective way by acquiring copies of the *Preparing for Adolescence* audio recordings by Dr. James Dobson or *Passport to Purity* by Dennis Rainey. They plan a weekend away—Mom with daughter or Dad with son or single parent with either sex—and drive someplace very special, such as a favorite campground, a shopping area, or whatever the child would enjoy. On the way there and back, parent and child listen to the recordings together, allowing Dr. Dobson or Dennis Rainey to say some difficult things in the hearing of both. This opens up dialogue between parent and child in ways never imagined. This dialogue is absolutely critical to preparing early adolescents for the changes they will experience over the coming months and years. You can get a *Preparing for Adolescence* kit from Focus on the Family (family.org) or the *Passport to Purity* kit from Family Life Ministries (familylife.com).

DATE NIGHTS

Every few weeks a father prepares for his date night. He gets spruced up and heads out to paint the town. But this date is not with his wife. It is with his teenage daughter. They are going to dinner and a movie. He will give his daughter tips on proper manners, how to act with boys, and why her purity is a priceless gift. An impression is made.

When parent-child date nights are a regularly scheduled activity on the calendar, Mom can take her son out to teach him how to treat a young girl with the respect and admiration she deserves. Or she can take her daughter out to discuss the fine art of appropriate flirting and behaving like a lady. Dad can help his son learn how to make himself look presentable and discuss how to talk to a girl. In these moments, all kinds of wonderful benefits occur, including planned and unplanned discussions.

MARRIED OR NOT?

When Kurt was young, his mother did something very wise while the family watched television together. Whenever there was a scene in which a man and woman became intimate with each other, Mom would tell them to turn the channel—but only if the couple was unmarried. If a married couple got frisky, on the other hand, they could watch the show. (Incidentally, this was in the days when television was far more discreet about what is actually shown on-screen.) In this small way, she made an important statement to help her kids discern that sex itself is not dirty or wrong unless experienced outside the context of marriage.

CHAPTER EIGHT

Instilling Faith

(Whatever You Do, Don't!)

Throughout this book we have done our best to provide parents with time-tested, proven strategies for messing up children's lives. Relying upon the seven downhill patterns of human depravity, you are now equipped with practical steps for accelerating their journey into misery, failure, and uselessness. You have also been cautioned about methods and activities that could place your children at risk of becoming happy and successful. We hope you have made note and taken appropriate precautions.

As we have explained, each of the deadly sins has a nemesis, some character virtue that works to undermine each vice. Parents might want to keep the following reference guide handy for "in the moment" decisions that inevitably arise. If faced with a situation in which you must decide between actively pushing a child uphill or passively allowing him or her to do what comes naturally, a quick glance at the following guidelines might prove useful.

MESS-UP PARENTING QUICK REFERENCE GUIDE

For Your Child's	Be Sure to . . .	Whatever You Do, Don't . . .
Attitude	Encourage pride	Nurture humility
Happiness	Inspire envy	Foster contentment
Temper	Provoke anger	Model self-control
Health	Feed gluttony	Demand temperance
Stuff	Fuel greed	Allow generosity
Work	Enable sloth	Require diligence
Desires	Condone lust	Expect chastity

With practice, selecting the best course of action will become more intuitive. Until then, however, keep this list of reminders handy.

The Greatest Risk

Despite a robust list of deadly sins serving as your mess-up tool kit, one category of parenting eclipses the rest when it comes to a parent's long-term influence on the next generation. It does not fit neatly into any of the topics addressed throughout this book, yet it touches each. You might even describe it as the foundation upon which all others rest. Namely, your child's faith.

We believe the most important strategy for messing up every area of a child's life is neglecting his or her faith formation. Put another way, the greatest risk to his or her long-term misery is the joy of knowing God.

Before discovering how, we should briefly review the "theology of kids" explained earlier.

Good News

In the opening scene of the Bible, we are given reason to be optimistic about the character of our children. We discover that "God created man in his own image, in the image of God he created him; male and female he created them" (Gen. 1:27).

Most Christians have heard that, as originally designed, man was created in the likeness of the Creator Himself. But what does this really mean? Do we mirror His physical likeness? Actually, as a Spirit, God does not have parts like a man. It rather means that we have a mental, moral, and social likeness, granting us the qualities and capacities that make us truly human.

In His mental likeness, we are able to reason and exercise our will. We are more than robotic computers, programmed to predetermined ends. We can think and choose. Animals are driven by instinctive urges. Humans can be guided by reasoned choices.

In His moral likeness, each of us has a conscience.

God is holy and compelled by His very nature to resist evil. In similar fashion, we are not morally passive but able to distinguish what is right from what is wrong, what is good from what is bad. Animals are driven by what feels right. Humans can know and choose what is right.

In His social likeness, we are able to love and relate to others. God has a social nature, motivating Him to create and love man. In like manner, we seek companionship, yearning to love and be loved by God and others. Animals can respond to others. Humans are able to truly love others.

So, as beings made after the likeness of God, our children possess some wonderful, awe-inspiring qualities.

Bad News

Now for the bad news. In the second scene of Genesis, we are given reason for a pessimistic view of human nature. You know the story. After giving access and dominion over everything on earth to mankind, God placed one restriction on Adam: not to eat from the tree of the knowledge of good and evil. The tempter came. The trap was set. The bait was offered. The sin was committed. Man broke the law, and the heart of his Creator. The deceiver stole away the heart of God's beloved. The human race chose the path of pain over the path of perfection.

How does the sin of Adam and Eve impact our children? Their choice has impacted every child born into the human race, including yours. As the apostle Paul wrote several hundred generations later: "All have sinned and fall short of the glory of God" (Rom. 3:23) and "Just as sin entered the world through one man, and death through sin, and in this way death came to all men, because all sinned" (Rom. 5:12).

The harsh truth we must face is that our children were not born with an innocent nature, prone toward good, but rather with a sinful nature, prone toward evil. In short, our kids have the same disease as the rest of us—sin.

Implications

The realities of human nature that form our theology of children also inform our theology of parenting. Drawing upon their truths, we can glean several implications for the process of teaching our children values or instilling vice.

> *Kid Reality #1:* Children have a rational, free will, giving them the capacity to understand and choose what is right; but because of a sinful nature, they will tend to choose what is wrong.
>
> *Parenting Implication:* We can hold our children responsible for their choices, teaching them to

counter their natural impulses (go uphill) or excuse them (go downhill).

Kid Reality #2: Children have consciences with which to distinguish right from wrong, but they can become callous to their consciences' urgings.

Parenting Implication: The way to help them develop and maintain informed, sensitive consciences is by consistently clarifying right from wrong and truth from error.

Kid Reality #3: Children have an inborn yearning for relationship with God but will resist and resent His or any other authority.

Parenting Implication: We will likely encounter resistance to our authority and instruction, requiring hard work and patience to teach kids what is right and good.

Kid Reality #4: Children are born with inherent worth and dignity, with tremendous capacity for good or evil.

Parenting Implication: Kids need a balance between knowing they are unconditionally loved as people with the conditional acceptance of their behavior.

To summarize, our children have been created in the likeness of God Himself, giving them tremendous potential and awe-inspiring qualities. But due to the Fall, they are prone toward evil and deception. Our job as parents is to understand the implications of these realities regardless of whether we intend to mess them up or fix them up.

Mess-Up Strategies

In light of these realities, mess-up parents implement one or more of the following strategies for ensuring a child's spiritual malnourishment.

MESS-UP STRATEGY #1: LEAVE IT TO THE PROS

The Bible instructs parents to be intentional about nurturing faith in their children. But mess-up parents adopt a different perspective. They believe we should leave such important work to the professionals. Pastors have seminary degrees. Priests get paid to lead religious instruction classes. Who are we as ordinary moms and dads to try tackling such an ominous task ourselves? We outsource their education to the schools, their music lessons to private instructors, and their athletic prowess to organized leagues. Why would we treat their faith formation any differently? Leave it to the pros. They know what they are doing.

MESS-UP STRATEGY #2: MINIMIZE CHURCH ATTENDANCE

Obviously, it would be easiest to simply avoid the church scene altogether. Sleeping in on Sundays is much, much easier than loading reluctant kids in the car and forcing them to sit through a worship service. But if you must go to church, do everything possible to minimize its impact by keeping faith on a surface level. Give them just enough religion to inoculate them from taking any of it very seriously.

MESS-UP STRATEGY #3: BE HAPHAZARD

As with any other area of success in life, helping children develop a strong faith requires purposeful intentionality. Moses wrote about this in Deuteronomy: "These commandments that I give you today are to be upon your hearts. Impress them on your children. Talk about them when you sit at home and when you walk along the road, when you lie down and when you get up" (6:6–7). The psalmist put it like this:

> He decreed statutes for Jacob
> and established the law in Israel,
> which he commanded our forefathers
> to teach their children,
> so the next generation would know them,
> even the children yet to be born . . .

Then they would put their trust in God
    and would not forget his deeds
    but would keep his commands.

                        (Psalm 78:5–7)

Moses and the psalmist knew what they were talking about when it came to spiritual training. So, whatever you do, ignore their advice.

MESS-UP STRATEGY #4: KEEP IT BORING

Christianity has some pretty exciting parts. But there is also plenty of boring stuff that can drive children away from Christian belief. If you talk about spiritual issues at all, be sure to do so in a somber, heavy tone to reinforce the notion religion is something we endure rather than enjoy. In this spirit, the activities listed at the end of this chapter are to be avoided at all costs!

Taking Precautions

Once again, instilling a strong Christian faith in our children can severely undermine our efforts to mess up their lives. That's why we encourage parents to ignore the following practical ideas intended to nurture belief.

> **WARNING:**
> *The following ideas could be hazardous to*
> *the process of messing up your child's life.*
> *Read at your own risk!*

GOD'S CHARACTER

When our children are very small (ages one to three), we imprint their lives by the way we treat them rather than by instructional activities. It is in this season that we impress their hearts, not their heads. Because children form their early view of God largely from how they view their parents, we can use the early years to reinforce the character of God—including both His love and His justice.

Love. When our children are very small, the best way to impress the love of God upon their hearts is by doing what comes naturally. We should overwhelm them with affirmation and affection, including lots of hugs and kisses, and praise for their fledgling attempts to talk, walk, and feed themselves. In these small ways, we are demonstrating unconditional love and the kind of affection God has for us. (By the way, don't stop as the child ages!)

Justice. In addition to establishing the security of unconditional love and affection when our children are very
small, it is important to establish a clear sense that
Mom and Dad set the rules and the child is expected to
obey those rules. Starting when your child is about
eighteen months old, establish a consistent system of
discipline when he or she willfully defies your rules.
We demonstrate God's character when we refuse to
tolerate rebellion against the rules we've established.

Please note, however, that there is a difference between willful defiance and childish irresponsibility.
Like God, we must clarify right from wrong with children and bring about appropriate discipline when rules
are violated. Parents who neglect this principle during
the early years risk giving children the mistaken idea
that love and justice are mutually exclusive. God is
both, and we must model both. Some excellent resources to help you implement this balance include
Dare to Discipline and *Hide or Seek*, both written by Dr.
James Dobson.

JUST LIKE AIR

Five-year-old Kyle and three-year-old Shaun stare at
Dad as he seriously contemplates the rather deep question he's just asked: "How can God be real if we can't
see Him?"

The oldest takes the lead. "That's a good question, Dad!"

"Well, is there anything else we know is real but we can't see?" asks Dad.

"How about air?" suggests Mom.

I pull out several balloons. We inflate them. "Air is real enough to expand these balloons. I bet air has power too," Dad says while releasing his balloon.

Now Shaun, the three-year-old, is really engaged! After ten minutes of intense competition over who can make their balloons fly farthest, Dad introduces a little slogan for tonight's activity: "Just like air, God is there!"

A lasting impression is made. In fact, ask either boy about how God can be real even though we can't see Him, and they will immediately respond, "Just like air, God is there!" Ask them what that means, and they'll explain: "God is real and has power, even though we can't see Him."

GOD MADE ALL THINGS

After reading the creation story in a children's picture Bible, pull out a large box of linking toys such as Legos or K'nex. Help the kids make several designs, such as people or cars or houses—whatever they like. After completing the "creation" process, take the creations apart and place the individual pieces on the floor. Ask, "How long do you think it will take for these pieces to put themselves back together without any help from us?"

The obvious answer—it will never happen.

Next, take the toy pieces and place them all in a bag or box. Ask the children to shake the bag or box and then dump the pieces on the floor. After the pieces fall randomly, express frustration. "I wanted them to fall into place to re-create the same designs we made before! Why didn't it work?" Try several times and keep expressing frustration that it doesn't work.

The kids will consider you silly—precisely what you want!

Pose the question, "How many times do you think it will take shaking and dumping before they become the designs again?"

The obvious answer—it will never happen.

Explain that many people believe the world simply made itself by chance rather than God's creating it on purpose. Just as you were silly to expect the toys to fall into place, it is silly to think our entire world made itself without a Creator!

LIGHT TO MY PATH

On a particularly dark evening, turn out every light in the house and enjoy a "light to my path" scavenger hunt with the kids. Create a list of things in the house that you need to find. Give the children flashlights or candles to light their path as they search for the various objects on your list. Once they have successfully gathered all the required items, reward them with a bowl of ice cream while you read Psalm 119:105 and compare your adventure with the scavenger hunt to how the Bible serves as a light as we navigate our way through life.

ONLY ONE WAY

In order to share that Jesus is the only way to God, try this simple activity. Have the kids attempt to roll a marble into a small jar or drinking glass from the top of a large piece of poster board. The board must remain straight during these first attempts. As they will discover, it is almost impossible to get the marble into the narrow head of the jar or glass. Next, turn the poster board over to discover a line drawn down the middle of the poster board with the name Jesus Christ written over the line. Help the child fold the poster board along the line, and then invite them to try rolling the marble into the jar or glass. Using the ravine created by the fold, it will be much easier to succeed.

Read Matthew 7:13–14 and John 14:6 and discuss Jesus' claim to be the only way to God. You may wish to recite a short rhyme to help your kids remember the principle: *Try as we may, there's only one way!*

*

Conclusion

On Second Thought

Confession time: we don't really recommend implementing any of the mess-up strategies outlined in this book. Sure, it's been fun wearing the devil's hat for a time. But we have no interest in raising little demons, and neither do you.

We decided to write the world's first guide to messing up a child's life in order to remind ourselves and other parents that it takes far less effort to instill vice than virtue, and that climbing "Mount Good Parents" requires much more effort than allowing our children to glide downhill. So, even though we become tired and sometimes complain about how hard parenting can be, deep down we know doing what's right will be worth it in the long run.

We have another confession: we are mess-up parents. That's because we are messed-up people. To paraphrase Romans 3:23: *All parents have messed up and fallen short of the perfection of God.* Truth be told, none of us do this job as well as we would like. We need to remember that, just like our kids, we parents struggle with the downward propensity of a fallen nature. It is difficult to help our children move uphill when we find our own feet sliding backward from time to time. The "theology of kids" we described earlier is also the theology of their parents.

Most of us worry that our inadequacies and failures will mess up our kids' lives. But we take comfort in another concept we learned back in Sunday school: the grace of God.

By God's grace, if you are doing the best you know how, you won't mess up your child's life. Oh, sure, you will make mistakes. And there are some moms and dads who do things that push children downhill rather than pull them up. But most of us try to do what's right most of the time.

Why, then, do so many children become such a mess as adults? Because each person has his or her own choices to make, and the scale of freedom remains tilted. Even those raised by saints can choose sin. But they can also turn from their propensity toward vice and head toward virtue.

You might say humanity's lingering image of God,

while imperfect, continues to offer every generation a reset button. No one has to live as victim to his or her upbringing. Countless souls raised in darkness have embraced the light of God's goodness.

Christianity is not a fatalistic faith. It is realistic, recognizing that the choices we make as parents will make it easier or harder for a child to reach his or her potential. That's why we must acknowledge our downhill propensity and turn the other way (repent) to climb uphill. Only then can we grab our children's hands to imperfectly pull them with us toward the joyous life we (and they) were made to know.

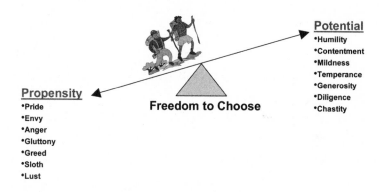

Our prayer is that your children will reap the blessings of parents who have the courage to do just that. We hope some of the ideas explored in this book prove helpful toward that end. Sure, you can parent without really trying. But we believe a little bit of intentionality will pay significant dividends in the lives of your children and grandchildren.

And so, with our fingers pointing up the slope, we humbly encourage you to start climbing!

While you're at it, why not dust off that idle exercise equipment?

Notes

INTRODUCTION: IT'S ALL DOWNHILL

1. Henry Fairlie, *The Seven Deadly Sins Today* (Notre Dame, IN: University of Notre Dame Press, 2005), 13.

CHAPTER 1: NURTURING AN ENORMOUS EGO

1. "The Dream," *Time*, March 22, 1963, http://www.time.com/time/magazine/article/0,9171,896687,00.html.

2. Ibid.

3. Found at http://en.wikipedia.org/wiki/Cassius_M._Clay.

4. Found at http://en.wikipedia.org/wiki/Muhammad_Ali.

5. "The Dream."

6. Ibid.

7. Found at http://en.wikipedia.org/wiki/The_Selfish_Gene.

8. *Webster's New World Dictionary of the American Language* (New York: Warner Books, 1984), 474.

9. Dr. James Dobson, *The New Strong-Willed Child* (Wheaton, IL: Tyndale House, 2004).

10. Fairlie, *Seven Deadly Sins*, 24.

11. Plato, *The Dialogues of Plato: Apology* (New York: Bantam Books, 1986), 8.

12. Ibid.

13. Ibid., 5.

CHAPTER 2: INSPIRING LASTING DISCONTENT

1. Peter Shaffer, *Amadeus* (New York: Harper & Row Publishers, 1980), 47.

2. Ibid., 49.

3. Ibid.

4. Ibid., 94.

5. William Shakespeare, *The Merchant of Venice* (3.2.115–16).

6. Solomon Schimmel, *The Seven Deadly Sins* (New York: Oxford University Press, 1997), 60–61.

7. Peter Kreeft, *Back to Virtue* (San Francisco: Ignatius Press, 1986), 121.

CHAPTER 3: ENCOURAGING AN EXPRESSIVE TEMPER

1. Found at http://en.wikipedia.org/wiki/Rabies.

2. Found at http://www.google.com/search?hl=en&defl=en&q=define:rabies&sa=X&oi=glossary_definition&ct=title.

3. Found at http://en.wikipedia.org/wiki/Mike_Tyson.

4. Fairlie, *Seven Deadly Sins*.

5. Kreeft, *Back to Virtue*, 138.

6. Ibid., 134.

7. Aristotle quoted by Ross W. Greene, PhD, *The Explosive Child* (New York: HarperCollins Publishers, 2001), vi.

8. Greene, *The Explosive Child*, 102–4.

9. Don Fleming, PhD, *How to Stop the Battle with Your Child* (New York: Prentice Hall Press, 1987), 137–39.

10. Dan Kindlon, PhD, *Too Much of a Good Thing* (New York: Hyperion, 2001), 97–98.

CHAPTER 4: FEEDING A VORACIOUS APPETITE

1. Found at http://www.msnbc.msn.com/id/14748549.

2. Found at http://www.rwjf.org/programareas/features/storieslist.jsp?year=2006&type=3&pid=1138.

3. Ibid.

4. Nanci Hellmich, "Obesity Can Run in Social Circles," *USA Today*, July 26, 2007.

5. Sandra G. Hassink, MD, *A Parent's Guide to Childhood Obesity* (Elk Grove Village, IL: American Academy of Pediatrics, 2006), xxiii.

6. Found at http://en.wikipedia.org/wiki/Seven_deadly_sins#Gluttony_.28Latin.2C_gula.29.

7. Found at http://www.stopaddiction.com/addiction/drug-abuse/substance_abuse_statistics.

8. Jeffrey Kluger, "The Science of Appetite," *Time*, June 11, 2007, 50.

9. Found at http://www.straightdope.com/columns/read/2421/were-there-really-vomitoriums-in-ancient-rome.

10. C. S. Lewis, *The Screwtape Letters* (New York: Bantam Books, 1982), 49.

11. Ibid.

12. Hassink, *Parent's Guide*, 9–12.

13. Dianne Neumark-Sztainer, PhD, *I'm, Like, So Fat!* (New York: Guilford Press, 2005), xi–xii.

14. Ibid.

CHAPTER 5: DISCOURAGING FRIVOLOUS GENEROSITY

1. Found at http://www.etymonline.com/index.php?search =avarice&searchmode=none.

2. *A Pocket Prayer Book for Orthodox Christians* (Englewood, NJ: The Antiochian Orthodox Christian Archdiocese, 1956), 29.

3. Adapted from the retelling in William J. Bennett, *The Book of Virtues* (New York: Simon & Schuster, 1993), 63–66.

4. Found at http://www.wordinfo.info/words/index/info/ view_unit/3870.

5. Reference reports found at http://people-press.org/ reports/print.php3?PageID=1145 and http://www.barna.org/ FlexPage.aspx?Page=BarnaUpdate&BarnaUpdateID=245.

6. Charles Dickens, *Christmas Books of Charles Dickens* (New York: Black's Readers Service, 1927), 43, 6–7.

7. Ibid.

8. Ibid., 30.

9. Ibid.

10. Ibid.

11. Ibid.

12. Fairlie, *Seven Deadly Sins*, 137–40.

13. Dickens, *Christmas Books*.

CHAPTER 6: FOSTERING TOTAL DEPENDENCE

1. Professor Masahiro Yamada, "The Age of Parasite Singles," http://en.wikipedia.org/wiki/Parasite_single.

2. Found at http://www.census.gov/population/socdemo/ hh-fam/tabMS-2.pdf.

3. Ruby K. Payne, PhD, *A Framework for Understanding Poverty* (Highlands, TX: aha! Process, Inc., 2005), 42–43.

4. M. Scott Peck, MD, *The Road Less Traveled* (New York: Simon & Schuster, 1978), 21–22.

5. Fairlie, *Seven Deadly Sins*, 123.

6. Ken Bazyn, *The Seven Perennial Sins and Their Offspring* (New York: Continuum International Publishing Group, 2004), 159.

7. Peck, *Road Less Traveled*, 19.

8. Found at http://www.procrastinationsupport.com/.

9. Bazyn, *Seven Perennial Sins*, 160.

10. Schimmel, *Seven Deadly Sins*, 193.

11. Bazyn, *Seven Perennial Sins*, 162.

12. Kreeft, *Back to Virtue*, 156.

13. *The Book of Common Prayer* (England: Oxford University Press, 1831), 8.

14. Found at http://en.wikiquote.org/wiki/John_Wesley.

15. Mark Rutland, *Behind the Glittering Mask* (Ann Arbor, MI: Servant Publications, 1996), 110.

CHAPTER 7: CONDONING SENSUAL GRATIFICATION

1. Ben Shapiro, *Porn Generation: How Social Liberalism Is Corrupting Our Future* (Washington, DC: Regnery Publishing, 2005), 28.

2. Schimmel, *Seven Deadly Sins*, 112.

3. Christopher West, *Theology of the Body for Beginners* (West Chester, PA: Ascension Press, 2004), 12.

4. Lewis, *Screwtape Letters*, 26.

5. Shapiro, *Porn Generation*, 28.

About the Bruners

Kurt and Olivia Bruner have four children. They are faculty members with The Center for Strong Families (www.strongfamilies.com) and host the HomePointe ministry (www.HomePointe.org). They are co-authors of *Playstation Nation*.

A graduate of Talbot Seminary, Kurt is a spiritual formation pastor at Lake Pointe Church who spent twenty years with Focus on the Family where he served as vice president overseeing creation of films, magazines, radio drama, and other practical tools for families. He is co-author of numerous books, including *Parents' Guide to the Spiritual Growth of Children*, *Your Heritage*, the Family Night Tool Chest series, and *Finding God in the Land of Narnia*.

A former schoolteacher, Olivia is the author of *The Minivan Years: Celebrating the Hectic Joys of Motherhood*. Learn more at www.BrunerWorld.com.